SOCIETY'S
CHILDREN

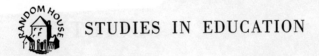

STUDIES IN EDUCATION

CONSULTING EDITOR:

PAUL NASH, *Boston University*

SOCIETY'S CHILDREN:

A Study of Ressentiment in the Secondary School

Carl Nordstrom
BROOKLYN COLLEGE

Edgar Z. Friedenberg
UNIVERSITY OF CALIFORNIA, DAVIS

Hilary A. Gold
BROOKLYN COLLEGE

RANDOM HOUSE *New York*

FIRST PRINTING

© Copyright, 1967, by Random House, Inc.

All rights reserved under International and Pan-American
Copyright Conventions. Published in New York by Random
House, Inc. and simultaneously in Toronto, Canada, by Random
House of Canada Limited

Library of Congress Catalog Card Number: 67–15464

Manufactured in the United States of America.
Composed by H. Wolff Book Manufacturing Co., N.Y.
Printed by Halliday Lithograph Corp., West Hanover, Mass.
Bound by The Colonial Press, Clinton, Mass.

Design by Kenneth Miyamoto

The wicked are wicked, no doubt, and they go astray
and they fall, and they come by their deserts; but who
can tell the mischief which the very virtuous do?

The Newcomes, William Makepeace Thackeray

Acknowledgments

WE DEEPLY APPRECIATE the support of the Cooperate Research Program of the Office of Education, U.S. Department of Health, Education, and Welfare, for the research reported herein. We also thank the College Entrance Examination Board for their help and supplementary financial assistance.

The authors are also indebted to Professor Hyman Sardy of Brooklyn College for his help in programming data and to the Office of Testing and Research at the College for processing the data. In addition, we gratefully acknowledge our debt to Professor Frank Peters of the State University of New York at Stony Brook for his technical assistance.

A special word of gratitude is due also to our graduate assistants, Walter Block and Melvin Fein, to our secretaries, Letty Eisenhauer, Crystal Hunter, Helen Kinzie, Marcia Tucker, and Linda Williams, and to our noble tape typists, who had to learn how to listen to the young respondents: Judith Dodson, Janet Francis, Carol Gordon, Muriel Herzog, Paul Kent, Elizabeth Lopuchin, Judith Partridge, and Ruth Silverman. Their diligence and devotion to duty were essential to the completion of this study.

Finally, our thanks to Estelle Fine, who worked on the manuscript. She was everything an editor should be, exacting, constructive in her criticism, and encouraging when courage was needed.

Contents

Tables

TEXT

APPENDIX A: PHASE I

APPENDIX B: PHASE II

Figure

SOCIETY'S
CHILDREN

Chapter I

A YOUNG MAN
NAMED HUGHES

WHEN GORDON HUGHES entered college in 1957 he hoped to become an engineer. This hope had developed out of his experience in high school where, he explained, he had found science and mathematics to be the only subjects that held his interest. "All the others," he added, "kept you well under wraps. You're pushed down to a level of mediocrity, and there's no chance to do anything more."

Hughes made this comment in response to the stock question, "Do you have anything more to say?" during a discussion of his change in major (from engineering to philosophy) while in his junior year in college. At that time, with his help and that of others, we were enquiring into the reasons why college students shifted from science majors into other fields.[1] Our procedure was designed to focus on college life, and normally respondents concentrated directly on that. If, in passing, they referred to their high schools, they generally stressed that they had been encouraged to major in science, and only that. It was the thing for a bright young man or woman to do.

Hughes' oblique comment on his negative experience in secondary school remained to nag us. Growing up, after all, is the primary work of youth, and our schools are the institutions through which

[1] See Carl Nordstrom and Edgar Z. Friedenberg, *Why Successful Students in the Natural Sciences Abandon Careers in Science* (New York: Brooklyn College, 1961).

this work is articulated. They are supposed to provide opportunities for the young to make something of themselves, and further, to serve as gateways into the society of success. They are also intended to serve the community, for it is through the school's work and the students' that the society is continually renewed. Further, education must be an enlarging experience, where as a matter of course enthusiasm and expressiveness join with discipline. It must be, it ought to be, but is it? Hughes' glum remarks suggest quite the opposite. Possibly they represent a unique experience and do not apply generally. As our findings developed, however, the concern inspired in us by Gordon Hughes' remarks intensified and grew sharper.

Research into reasons for leaving the natural sciences led us to two general conclusions. The first was that for many students science had turned out to be a grind. Again and again respondents described the scientific activity they had encountered as routine drudgery, with the moments of excitement and discovery few and far between. As they saw it the average scientist could expect to spend most of his life hammering away at a narrowly defined task without ever having much opportunity to develop a real feeling for the overall purpose of his work. Furthermore, we found such observations to be as true for students who had continued in science as they were for those who, after having had a fling at science, had decided on some other career.

A striking contrast between those who stayed with science and those who had left for other pursuits led us to our second conclusion. While most respondents described science as primarily drudgery, this had not deterred some from continuing with a scientific career. These individuals, who served as a control group during the science dropout research, all had very high academic averages. They were further characterized by a willingness to work very hard, a willingness they carried as if it were a badge of honor, and since they took a certain pride in their monkhood, their contempt for their less committed fellows was not always veiled.

On the other hand, they showed little or no curiosity, either about their science or themselves. In fact, despite their exceptional performance in college, they were not given much to thinking about anything. They were polite, conscientious, duty-bound, proud in their suffering, . . . and that was that. One such respondent is described by Friedenberg in *Coming of Age in America* as lacking "a sense of personal authority, even over himself" and, further along, as one who "is driven by humility rather than ambition." [2] In general our continuants seemed unable to imagine any real alternative to the values and assumptions they had grown up with. For these reasons we came to think of them as conventional.

Among the students who had left science were many who resembled in their outlook those who had continued with natural science. There was also, however, a statistically identified cluster of subjects who stood polarly opposite to the conventionally minded. While their academic averages, around B, were not high when compared with the continuants, their verbal-intellectual performance was of a different order entirely. They had thought—and were still thinking deeply—about science. They were also able to discuss it brilliantly, and did, at length. Though less successful academically, they clearly were far better educated than the continuants. They were also concerned with personal self-integration and the maintenance of a healthy spirit of inquiry and had come to see a scientific education as an impediment to this concern. Gordon Hughes, the archetype of this group, described his change to philosophy in these words,

There were two circles—my studies and my interests. Now I have one and it's a considerably bigger circle. I have an awful lot of interests, but somehow they all tie in, and I feel this. I mean, it's just round; it's nice, inner calm, peace, and perfectly satisfied.

Philosophy is hardly very practical, but it ties his life together; most of these young men and women were *not* practical, they had given this up in their search for integrity. We came to think of them as adolescents because they exhibited the exuberance and optimism of youth.

In a sentence, then, the conventionals were still in science and making progress toward their degrees; the adolescents had strayed

[2] Edgar Z. Friedenberg, *Coming of Age in America* (New York: Random House, 1965), p. 24.

elsewhere, and, if the figure of speech makes any sense, had strayed with a vengeance.

Superficially, as this process continues, those who can adjust will surely be the scientists of the future. Undoubtedly, most of them will serve well on the assembly lines of science. Their craftsmanship will be uniformly excellent if not creative. Society will accept them in their willingness to respond to its conventions and reward them with authority.

The adolescents, for their part, if they continue on the course they have chosen, will end up out of science altogether. They will not have the prerequisites necessary for a scientific career. Eventually, many will work themselves into something worthwhile, but some will certainly find it exceedingly difficult to settle down. Locked in self-absorption, craving sensation, afflicted with ennui, their stray will turn to drift. For a few the drift will be funereal, a pathetic alienation from life itself. Such talented young men and women, out of sorts with this world and unable to muster up their resourcefulness, are only too commonplace as misery figures in our age.

Some observers, like Talcott Parsons, might take comfort in our society's continued and possibly increasing success in producing the duty-bound such as our continuants turned out to be.[3] Others, however, may notice an ominous implication in these findings: for it is those who have dared to take a fling at adolescence who drop out from science. And, if Erik Erikson is correct in his judgments about the function of creative youth, we then face a potential disaster for society as well as a series of personal tragedies. In his article "Youth, Fidelity and Diversity," he writes,

> It is the young, who by their responses and actions, tell the old whether life as represented by the old and as presented to the young has meaning; and it is the young who carry in them the power to confirm those who confirm them and joining the issues, to renew and to regenerate, or to reform and to rebel.[4]

[3] Talcott Parsons, "Youth in the Context of American Society," in *The Challenge of Youth,* ed. by Erik H. Erikson (New York: Anchor Books, 1965), pp. 110-141. See esp. pp. 139-140.

[4] Erik H. Erikson, "Youth: Fidelity and Diversity," in *The Challenge of Youth,* p. 24.

Such renewal and such reinvigoration demand of the young fidelity and a capacity for diversity. Of these qualities Erikson writes in summarizing,

> Fidelity, when fully matured, is the strength of disciplined devotion. It is gained in the involvement of youth in such experiences as reveal the essence of the era they are to join—as the beneficiaries of its tradition, as the practitioners and innovators of its technology, as renewers of its ethical strength, as rebels bent on the destruction of the outlived, and as deviants with deviant commitments.[5]

Is not the practice of science, in its most noble sense, just such an innovation, such a destroying, such a joining of issues? Does it not require fortitude, fidelity, passion, and discipline, and in exactly the manner Erikson describes? And if this is what science requires, how well equipped are the young people who participated in the science study to reform or to rebel, to renew and to regenerate?

Poorly, we think. In terms of their outlook it was the adolescents we encountered who came closest to the ideal. They did seek to understand and did throw their world into question. But this distracted them and, unable or indifferent to developing the necessary discipline, they left for other fields. If they do eventually achieve such self-discipline, they will, unfortunately, have achieved it too late to be of service in the practice of science. The conventionals for their part were dutiful. They accepted but did not question. They were also docile. Many had proved themselves capable of the discipline Erikson demands and were progressing with distinction toward their degree. However, while the community confirmed them, their own individuality did not. Often lumpish or insipid, they were lacking in an indignation that could have served wholeness, and so remained a sack of parts. With little passion for devotion to anything but amenities, they were weak in creative energy. Both the adolescent and the conventional styles are flawed, we maintain; both are incomplete in that each needs something of its polar opposite if it is to do great things. And great things are what we are talking about.

[5] *Ibid.,* pp. 22-23.

At the conclusion of the science study, then, we were left with this question to ruminate over: given that these two styles are incommutable, is there something noxious about the common social experience of these young men and women that forces them into the blind alleys they inhabit?

It was at this point that Gordon Hughes and his disquieting description of high school came back to mind, for it reminded us of a social process elucidated earlier in the century by the German phenomenologist, Max Scheler. Should it be active in the school environment, it would without a doubt be sufficiently noxious to devitalize youth. This was the process *ressentiment*.

Ressentiment, which sounds like a French translation of the word "resentment," approximates its meaning only imprecisely. A term first introduced by Friedrich Nietzsche in *The Genealogy of Morals* and subsequently elaborated in Scheler's *Ressentiment*,[6] ressentiment is less completely conscious than ordinary resentment and less focused on the particular experiences that are its actual causes, and it is more of a social than a psychological phenomenon. In contrast to conventional resentment, ressentiment is usually rationalized, covert, diffuse, and largely unconscious. Just as one may legitimately refer to "free-floating anxiety" as a decisive element in certain kinds of personality, ressentiment is a kind of free-floating ill temper. Scheler characterizes ressentiment as "a lasting mental attitude, caused by the systematic repression of certain emotions and affects which, as such, are normal components of human nature." "Their repression," he goes on to say, "leads to the constant tendency to indulge in certain kinds of value delusions and corresponding value judgments"; the "emotions and affects primarily concerned are revenge, hatred, malice, envy, the impulse to detract, and spite." [7] Lewis Coser, in his introduction to Scheler's work, adds that to Nietzsche ressentiment is a central concept in his so-

[6] Friedrich Nietzsche, *The Birth of Tragedy* and *The Genealogy of Morals,* trans. by Francis Golffing (Garden City, N. Y.: Anchor Books, 1956). Golffing translates the word *ressentiment* as rancor. See also Max Scheler, *Ressentiment*, trans. by William W. Holdheim, with an introduction by Lewis A. Coser (Glencoe: The Free Press, 1961).

[7] Scheler, *Ressentiment,* pp. 45-46.

cial psychology . . . a basic component of "that slave morality to which he counterposed his master morality." [8]

Now let us return again to Gordon Hughes, certainly an intelligent, imaginative young man, at one time a scientist in his dreams. If we add a touch of ressentiment to the leavening of his high school life, what happens then? The essential quality of the creative student, as he is beginning to be defined in the literature, is that his thought is divergent.[9] He doesn't arrive at "right" answers by deducing them from established premises, but by an intuitive understanding of how the problem he is dealing with really works, of what actually goes into it. He works hard when the problem requires it and respects facts as a part of reality. But, for the creative students, facts are not simply right answers but tools and components for building original solutions.

Faced with the potentially creative student, with our hypothetical Hughes, how will the secondary school teacher react? If he is a high school teacher because the job gives him joy and if he is competent intellectually, he will react with delight. But to the degree that he is ressentient, his reaction will be permeated with defensive hostility. Consider, for example, the poor mathematician who somehow manages to salvage enough math to become a high school teacher. Such a teacher functions by knowing a set of answers and a conventional procedure for arriving at them. He maintains his self-esteem by convincing himself that this is enough; the student like Hughes who confronts him and who really understands mathematics puts him in a dilemma. On the one hand, a Hughes may show up his teacher as incompetent. On the other, the teacher may suspect the student of conning him and even of laughing at him for being taken in. Caught in a bind the teacher dares not commit himself to either interpretation. If he is an authoritarian, he bullies the student into solving the problems "the way I show you as long as you are in my class." If he is "philanthropic," he re-

---

[8] *Ibid.,* p. 21.

[9] J. P. Guilford, "The Structure of Intellect," *Psychological Bulletin,* 53 (July, 1956), 267-293. See also Jacob W. Getzels and Philip W. Jackson, *Creativity and Intelligence* (New York: John Wiley, 1962), *passim.*

sponds with studied tolerance and amusement to the "attention-getting behavior" of a Hughes. But in either case the teacher tries to make sure that Hughes doesn't embarrass him again by actually getting up and doing mathematics in front of the whole class.

At mathematics, though, a Hughes can win, and for that reason he has something he can feel good about. After all, there are right answers. This helps explain the difference in his feelings about math and science from his feelings about the other subjects.

In the humanities and in the social studies the creative student is both more threatening and more vulnerable. He is more vulnerable because there aren't any right answers to support him. He is more threatening because these subjects, if truthfully handled, are in themselves threatening to the ressentient. It is the job of the humanities and the social sciences to get to the root of human experience, which at best means hewing austere beauty out of some very ugly blocks in such a way that their real character is revealed. This is just what ressentiment cannot tolerate. And this is what makes both the humanities and social studies so dangerous in the classroom, for to teach them well is to inquire directly into the essence of human experience.

So much for Gordon Hughes and his trials. By now he should have completed his wanderings in the groves of academe and, hopefully, has embarked on new ventures in the larger world. But his oblique reference to his experience in secondary school remained to haunt us. It started us thinking.

This book is the product of that thought and the research attendant on it. Here we seek to determine whether there might be an unrecognized process by which schools actually do something *to* students, and in the doing, seriously interfere with the development of what used to be called a strong and forceful character.[10] We thought that this process might be ressentiment, as defined by Nietzsche and Scheler, and this thought has guided our research. In our preliminary judgment ressentiment operated to stifle enthusiasm, to undermine fortitude, and to discourage the development of self-mastery; and to the degree that this is true we saw ressentiment

[10] John Dewey, *Moral Principles in Education* (New York: Philosophical Library, 1959). See pp. 49-50.

as insidious when endured, difficult to fight, and stultifying in its consequences.

We also thought that this process was not only unrecognized, but, in a formal sense, unintended. And, to the degree that this is true, we felt it should be brought to the attention of responsible persons.

Chapter II

THE RESEARCH
PROTOCOL

THE EXISTENCE OF any social system implies the existence of an institutional press. This press is the unique set of modes by which the system seeks to bend the individuals participating in the system to its demands. A school is such a system. Examples of such modes in a school include the requirement that all pupils must be in attendance in their home rooms at some stated time and the teacher's action *qua* teacher in calling the role to make certain that the pupils have complied with this requirement. Operating through existing prescriptions and procedures and experienced either as an alien force or internalized as super-ego direction, the press expresses the system's claim to authority over the individual. In its impositions, an institutional press can be direct or subtle, it can be helpful, even heartwarming, or, should this be necessary, it can be willful, it can be cruel. And, to the degree that an individual bends and adjusts to the pressures of an institution, to that degree these pressures, reified as the press, cooperate in the making of his character. Needless to say, their effects can be both good and bad.

Basic to this investigation are three propositions related to schools as institutional presses. They are: (1) that ressentiment is an important element in the institutional press of secondary schools; (2) that it differs in intensity and scope from school to school (As we began our research, we expected to find differences in school ressentiment to be scaled along social class dimensions; Nietzsche's critical distinction between master and slave moralities suggested that ressentiment would be most intense and most noxious in lower class schools with middle class teachers, and least intense in public and private schools with an upper class orientation.); and (3) that ressentiment has unwholesome consequences for the young people attending schools where its influence prevails.

What, then, is ressentiment? To Scheler, ressentiment begins when an angry individual feels an oppressive sense of impotence which he cannot imagine actively transcending.[1] This impotence results from his having lost out in competition with others over the course of his life. Angry, as a result of his failure, he retains a desire for revenge, a desire that stands in conflict with his essential impotence. This produces in him a tension which, in a dangerous world, must remain secret and, yet, if he is to be at peace with himself, must somehow be resolved. Resolution comes, according to Scheler, through an extraordinary value transformation, a self-delusion whereby the individual afflicted makes a virtue of his predicament by substituting values consistent with it for those alien to it. In this act he derogates what Scheler calls "vital values" such as those of well-being, health, beauty, freedom; in short, values associated with youth, with growth, and with authentic maturity. Such values he either condemns, ignores, or replaces in his act of transformation with values derived from weakness and fear. As a result he transforms his failure into a moralized success.

Essentially, ressentiment is a value pose, a technique for distinguishing the good from the bad. Evoked, it assumes weakness. It both seeks and proffers pity and tries always to be helpful. Thus, the style of ressentiment is philanthropic, for this is safe, but philanthropic with a twist. This is because its primary object is to damage. Alone, in the hands of a single individual, it is little more than the bad temper of a failure sweetened for his public and exists only as personal misery. When endemic in society, however, ressentiment is a formidable evil, for, despite the often-assumed pose of tender sorrow, it is rooted in malevolence. Hatefulness, masked as understanding and affection, is the dark undertone of its meaning.

It was Nietzsche's concern, and Scheler's too, that the ressentient, when working insidiously and in concert, would distort the

---

[1] See Max Scheler, *Ressentiment,* trans. by William W. Holdheim (Glencoe: The Free Press, 1961), *passim.*

values of any group they dominated. A form of ressentiment pertinent to such a condominium is suggested by Jean-Paul Sartre, who describes "men of resentment" as individuals who by their very subjectivity "establish their human personality as a perpetual negation." [2] One who is ressentient in this way refuses to bring the Other he deals with into focus as an individual. Instead he will only do business with abstract entities—such as with teen-agers or troublemakers, not with John or Mary. In this way, threatening individuality is kept in its place, danger is circumvented, and mass values are upheld. To the degree that such abstracting can be justified as being "for your own good," and it often can be for those who want to fit in, the philanthropic element in ressentiment is retained. "Someday, you will thank me for what I have done," the man says as he gives out detention to a student—and what may be a furtive vengeance becomes thereby a triumph of virtue.

This illustration, drawn from Sartre, indicates a form of ressentiment manifested as instituted practice and also suggests the difficulty inherent in measuring its intensity in an institutional setting. Although the rules and practices of a school may have been deliberately framed to facilitate ressentiment, they are not in themselves a sufficient cause of ressentiment. For one thing, the rules may be ignored by those in authority, and for another, the detention mentioned above could have been deserved. In this particular case it was the sanctimonious explanation that revealed the spirit of the act, not the act itself. Because of such difficulties in examining instituted practices and processes for evidence of ressentiment—our object in what we term Phase I of the study—we can approach our phenomena only tentatively.

Central to our efforts at measuring the incidence of ressentiment in the schools that participated in this study is a 75-item index, which we (Friedenberg and Nordstrom) modeled after the index of institutional press characteristics that was developed by Pace and Stern[3] and which we focused specifically on ressentient practices

[2] Jean-Paul Sartre, *Being and Nothingness*, trans. and with an introduction by Hazel E. Barnes (New York: Philosophical Library, 1965), p. 47.

[3] C. Robert Pace and George Stern, *A Criterion Study of College*

and attitudes. A copy of our instrument, the Friedenberg-Nordstrom Ressentiment Index—identified throughout as the F-N *R* Index—together with its key and resulting test data are included as Appendix A, Part I, of this work.[4]

The standard item in the F-N *R* Index is an affirmative statement which the respondent scores either true or false depending on whether or not it is perceived as characteristic of his high school. Item (45), for example, states, "You have to be concerned about marks here, that is, if you are going to get anywhere and be anything." This is keyed true, that is, the item is held to manifest ressentiment, because the student is encouraged to think first of his future and only derivatively of himself. To the degree that this prescription carries force in his school he must face up to the power of grades and adjust to what they imply. His worth to himself is determined by what he will become, not by what he is, and thus he establishes himself in his negation. In schools where this attitude prevails, marks do more than signify; they also make possible such individuality as is possible there.

Support for the validity of these observations is offered by a respondent from the high school we have named Milgrim.[5] Miss Svensen is a lovely young lady who always dresses tastefully. She is clearly not a troublemaker for trouble's sake alone. During a discussion conducted by Professor Friedenberg with several Milgrim students, Miss Svensen said, in a quiet but serious manner,

> You're taught to put aside your own interests and have an interest in reading or something like that. You're taught to put aside your own interests and do what's important.

After comments by other participants, such as "what *they* feel is important," Miss Svensen continued,

---

Environment (New York: Syracuse University Research Institute, 1958).

[4] It is suggested that the reader review this section (pp. 149-64) for better comprehension of what follows.

[5] Except for technical references and cited authors, all names of persons and places are fictitious.

> Everyone has to take the same path. It's so mapped out, you have to take the same path as everybody else. . . . It's difficult for all but a very smart person to take a path of his own.

And further along she broke in again,

> Even though we talk of being different, as we would like to be, for whatever reason, you just feel that the only reward is in doing the set thing. . . . You feel truly that you have to be—that you have to do what's mapped out for you or else there's no. . . . That's the true path of your responsibility and that you should be actually doing it. It's the life that you were born into, it's your responsibility, . . . if you're different, you're just not accepting your responsibility.

A victim of some abstract "they" that is beyond her control, Miss Svensen finally comes to terms with this "they" authority, accepting it as a true expression of what ought to be. Thus, she surrenders her hopes for individuality, but still, she wonders, is not something amiss here?

On the F-N *R* Index, either a true or a false answer can be keyed as evidence of ressentiment. An example of a false-as-ressentiment item is (46), "If a boy and a girl go steady here, the chances are that they are really in love." Few young people, it seems, believe that their contemporaries are capable of real love, for 80 percent of all students scored this item false. Our teacher subjects, at 96 percent, were even more emphatic in rejecting the statement. The implication is clear that strong, close, affectionate feelings are not to be expected in high school students and that what love there is must be puppy love. Of all items, this item generated the strongest false-as-ressentiment response, and Item 45—previously cited as an example of a true-as-ressentiment item—the strongest for its category. Better than 90 percent of all student respondents marked it true.

With Scheler's delineation of ressentiment in mind, we (Friedenberg and Nordstrom) each wrote forty such items and then pruned and edited the other's work. This was in keeping with a central principle of method that we have evolved in working together, which we term "task independence." Recognizing at the outset our differences as persons, we seek to exploit these differences rather than to mediate them through a consensus. For this reason we organize our efforts as separate tasks. After working on these tasks independently we each cross-check our results against the other's. Such task independence, we feel, introduces an element of objectivity into the research, and for that reason we utilize it wherever possible.

An example of a different application of task independence was our use of part of the Stern High School Characteristics Index, an instrument originally designed to test many aspects of a high school institutional press. A section of this index was adapted for ressentiment testing simply by constructing a special key for it. This section, here called the Stern *R* Index, consists of sixty items which we selected because we agreed they could be keyed true- or false-as-ressentiment. Professor Gold, although not originally a member of the study team, joined us in making up this key. We added the sixty items to the testing protocol as a check to insure against a built-in bias in the seventy-five items we had written ourselves. As statistical comparisons indicated that the two instruments (given one after the other as a unit of 135 items) agreed well in their assessment of the overall response, we have generally followed the practice of adding the scores of both indexes together and reporting them as a combined score.[6]

Professor Gold's role is another example of task independence. Besides helping with the adaptation of part of the Stern Index, he joined the study to assess the institutional press in the several schools in terms of ressentiment using means other than those al-

[6] The items were chosen among numbers (91) to (180) of the Stern Index. As it is used widely in assessing schools and confidentiality about its contents is necessary, we have not reproduced these items or the school-by-school response to them as we have with the F-N *R* Index in Appendix A, Part I. Professionally qualified persons can obtain copies of the Stern instrument from the Psychological Research Center, Syracuse University. A statistical comparison of results for the two instruments can be found in Carl Nordstrom, Edgar Z. Friedenberg, and Hilary A. Gold, *Influence of Ressentiment on Student Experience in Secondary School,* Coop. Research Project No. 1758 (New York: Brooklyn College, 1965), p. 9 and p. 134. Hereafter, when cited, this report will be identified as The Project Report, CRP 1758.

ready devised. This he did in several ways. First, in making arrangements with the schools and supervising Phase I testing, he experienced the organization itself. He also observed classes in session at each school, coffee-klatched with faculty and students, and collected whatever material the schools published about themselves. Student handbooks, for instance, turned out to be a most useful source of information about the school's vision of its function. Finally, he added two other instruments to the Phase I testing protocol: (1) what we came to call the Best Thing-Worst Thing Test, in which the subject was asked to describe briefly the best thing that has ever happened to him in high school and also the worst thing; and (2) a Non-Verbal Perception Test, in which the respondent was asked to draw an ideal social studies classroom.

For Phase I testing, in which we attempted to measure the ressentiment component present in the institutional presses of several schools, and, thus, to test propositions (1) and (2)[7] the protocol for the study specified that a sample group of 100 students and from 5 to 7 teachers be drawn from each school. All participation in the research was voluntary, and all subjects were paid for their consultation work with the project. In our preliminary discussion with the schools we asked that the selected students be chosen at random—that every nth name be taken from an alphabetical listing of the total school population in Grades 10, 11, and 12. We also asked that the selected teachers should, if possible, be chosen from those in policy-making positions in school. In working through this protocol, however, scheduling and other administrative difficulties developed from time to time, and the ideal is only approximate for each school. In all, 902 students and 57 teachers distributed over 9 schools served as subjects for Phase I testing.

In concert with the object of Phase I testing, we also attempted to measure the impact of ressentiment-infected environments on the students attending those schools. This procedure, in which we test the third proposition, we termed Phase II. Presumably, if our basic propositions are correct, differences in ressentiment will be reflected in differences in the students according to the particular school press in which the ressentiment is prevalent. In general, we

[7] Our findings in reference to proposition (2) are reported in Appendix A, Part II.

expected salient value orientations that had been conspicuous in the science study to reassert themselves. That is, we anticipated a conglomerate structure composed of *conventionals,* similar to the continuants of the science study; *adolescents,* like Gordon Hughes in their enthusiasm and unevenness; and *residual* types, distinguished by idiosyncratic value preferences. All these, merged together with others, taxonomically vague, into a general mass, would constitute the population of students.

We understood conventionals to be those who generally accept the institution and its conventions. Predisposed towards the leadership of the instituted authorities, formal or informal, adult or peer, they would tend to reduce conflicts to stereotyped terms and to prefer instrumental ends to those concerned with their own vitality and integrity. This deportment would be manifested in a strong desire to please and a low degree of personal-emotional involvement in the current predicament, with the combination often expressing itself as resignation.

Adolescents, to us, were students whose primary concern was with the meaning of their own identity. Their relationship to authority would be provisional, as much demanding as respectful; competent craftsmanship rather than status—in Fromm's terms "rational authority"—would command their approbation.[8] As they seek primarily to establish themselves in a clear relationship with their own feelings as well as with their society, they will give much evidence of being self-absorbed.

Residuals, for their part, were expected to be heterogeneous aggregates of individuals and small groups. Authoritarianism, consistent and undiscriminating hostility towards all types of authority, or patterns of stereotypy peculiar to individual schools are what we had in mind. Riesman's category "anomic" also helps to describe them.[9]

For Phase II testing we developed a set of six related, forced-choice, Q-sort tests, tests in which a situation is described where

[8] Erich Fromm, *Man for Himself: An Inquiry into the Psychology of Ethics* (New York: Holt, Rinehart & Winston, 1947), p. 9.
[9] David Riesman, with Nathan Glazer and Reuel Denney, *The Lonely Crowd: A Study of the Changing American Character* (New Haven: Yale University Press, 1961), pp. 243-245.

some kind of problem is posed. In Q-sort testing, following the description are prepared comments, from which the subject must choose those he deems most suitable and those least suitable for the situation. Through this forced choosing he, theoretically, reveals his attitudes. The letter "Q" is used conventionally to designate such forced-choice testing procedures.[10]

For each of the six tests we devised, the subject was given an episode to read and was then asked to respond in terms of nine prescribed comments. He was asked to select the three comments he most preferred, and of these "good," the one he considered Best. He was then to choose the three he most deplored and from these "poor," the one he deemed Worst. The three remaining comments constituted those he considered "neutral." [11] We hypothesized that clusters generated by these tests would have characteristics associated with the ressentiment content of the school's institutional press.

An example of such an episode is *The Clarke-Barto Incident*. This describes an event in the school life of Mr. Arthur Clarke, a social studies teacher. Clarke is described as having just entered a men's washroom where he encounters a surly youth who is smoking. This young man, Johnny Barto, is known around the school as a troublemaker. In addition, the instructions state that the school is strict about enforcing the rule against smoking. With this information the respondent is asked to distribute from best to worst the nine comments, each on individual cards, each one of which specifies an action which Mr. Clarke might take when faced with Johnny's delinquency. Of the nine, the most popular card was the eighth one. It reads,

[10] For a comprehensive discussion of Q-sort testing see William Stephenson, *The Study of Behavior, Q-Technique and Its Methodology* (Chicago: The University of Chicago Press, 1953).

[11] The complete text of the six episodes and their cards, along with tables reporting results, are presented in Appendix B. A comprehensive discussion of the responses can be found in Edgar Z. Friedenberg, *Coming of Age in America* (New York: Random House, 1965), pp. 51-154. These responses play a central role in the author's discussion of student values in that work.

At the faculty meeting that afternoon, Mr. Clarke discusses the "Johnny Barto problem" with the school psychologist, and the school psychologist agrees to set up a counseling program designed to get at Johnny's "antisocial" behavior and straighten him out. The psychologist then calls Johnny in for counseling.

The ninth card was the most unpopular,

Mr. Clarke acts as if he hadn't noticed Johnny and leaves the washroom as soon as possible.

The seven other choices are: (1) The two get into a fight. (2) Clarke coolly beats Johnny up. (3) Johnny is made an example of for Clarke's social studies class. (4) Johnny is sent to the principal. (5) Johnny is remanded to the Student Court. (6) Clarke calls Johnny's parents. And (7) Johnny is made to write lines on the blackboard during a detention. In effect the respondent is given a choice from among actions which humiliate Johnny, straighten him out, remand him to other authorities, or ignore his transgression altogether. On completion the respondent's pattern of choices is recorded.

The Q-sort episodes increase in complexity from the first to the sixth (*Clarke-Barto* is the first) and touch on a variety of situations relative to the school. Subjects completed two episodes per day for three days. Each day's testing was followed immediately by an interview. The interviews were as nondirective as possible, taking their theme from the responses given. In many cases two or more students were interviewed together.

Again, following the principle of task independence, we divided our procedure into separate tasks. We (Friedenberg and Nordstrom) each wrote three of the episodes, one for each day. Friedenberg did all of the interviewing, taping them as he went along. Nordstrom listened to the interviews on audio tape, edited the typescript, and annotated them extensively. At the same time he processed the quantitative results of the testing. These data, the annotated typescript, and the direct experiences of one of the investigators became the basis for our Phase II analysis, our assessment of the impact of ressentiment on the student subjects.

Our protocol for Phase II specified that a sample of 25 pupils be drawn from the Phase I sample of 100 at each school. Again, to obtain a cross section of student opinion, the nth-name randomizing technique was used to obtain these twenty-five. In addition, all teachers in Phase I were asked to participate in an abridged Phase II to the extent of answering the set of Q-sort tests (Episodes III and IV) given on the second day.

In the course of collecting data, we expanded the sample for Phase II beyond what had been originally specified by the protocol. Our experiences in the first schools that we visited led us to conclude that the randomly produced cross section of opinion was of a massive single mind and decidedly inarticulate. To compensate we added subjects to the sample in a manner almost consciously unsystematic—we went out to look for subjects who might have something to say. Several such subjects were nominated by the schools themselves, especially in cases where teachers expressed an interest in how particular students whom they personally considered "different" would fare on the test. In other instances the project investigators added subjects, choosing from among respondents with exceptionally high or low R index scores during Phase I testing. At Ipswich a boy vigorously attacked the project, posting an open letter on the school bulletin board. He was added for this reason. And finally, one ambitious young man at Parma surreptitiously included himself in the sample. Oddly enough, this latter boy, who thought of himself as highly original, turned out to be among the most conventional respondents of all.

There are eighteen of these auxiliary subjects. Generally they enrich the response. They do, however, introduce a statistical bias, for the results of the Q-sort testing tend, through their influence, to overstate the heterodoxy of the respondents. In all, 245 students, including these 18 auxiliaries, and 55 teachers participated in Phase II testing for the study.

To recapitulate briefly, we have followed Scheler and Nietzsche closely in defining ressentiment. When beginning the study, we hypothesized that students in schools which are highly ressentient would adapt themselves to institutional roles and procedures under this pressure or would retreat into defensive postures such as open hostility, incompetence, or indifference. Phase I testing was designed to measure ressentiment in the schools; Phase II testing was designed to assess its impact on the students. We expected the data to support the inference that ressentiment in schools operates to transform adolescents, by whom we mean young people who are seriously concerned with self-understanding and the development of their potentials, into conventionals, by whom we mean role players of some efficiency, or into residuals, which covers a variety of anomic and semi-anomic respondents. Ressentiment, that is, makes people inauthentic. Should our findings bear this out, ressentiment would have been shown to stultify secondary school students and, consequently, to be an unwholesome influence.

Chapter III

TWO MIDDLE-MIDDLE
SCHOOLS IN
A STATE OF FLUX

From our Phase I testing we wished to assess secondary schools in terms of ressentiment. To achieve this object we prepared a profile description of each of the schools participating in the study, using the material we had gathered. Our primary source of information was our respondents themselves, by means of their answers to the ressentiment index and the Best Thing-Worst Thing Test. (A more abstract assessment of the several schools, phrased in terms of socioeconomic factors, educational practices, and ressentiment scores has also been prepared and can be found in Appendix A, Part II, of this work. A review of this material in conjunction with the reading of the several profiles is recommended.) In articulating the profiles, here, we have concentrated on isolating the ressentiment element in the institutional press. For this reason the schools emerge in sharper delineation than they might have were the concern a balanced statement in the conventional sense.

Nine secondary schools—seven public and two independent schools—participated in this study. They were selected because they differed in terms of sociological characteristics and also because they were willing to undergo examination. Two of the nine, the two profiled in this chapter, are so categorically central in every sociological sense that they can be most aptly described, using Lloyd Warner's terms, as middle-middle class. The first to be profiled is Parma, so named in honor of its vague resemblance to a certain charterhouse.

PARMA HIGH SCHOOL

I think the worst thing that happened to me in Parma was facing and accepting the problems of growing up. We all realize that we will have to face them soon, we might even be facing them now. Basically these problems confront us at Parma, socially rather than educationally.

A Parma Student

The school district which Parma High School serves is scenic, suburban, and comfortable, almost affluent. At $7,977 its median family income is second highest for the seven public schools included in this study (see Table 1, p. 166). Comparatively speaking, Parma's parents have good jobs, with over one third of the males working in professional, technical, and managerial positions. Among the occupations reported for the fathers of Parma's students were chemist, writer, and sales manager, as well as barber, welder, and custodian. Parma parents are above average for the sample in educational attainment as well, with 29 percent having completed one or more years of college.

Ambivalence concerning its past and its present typifies Parma; the high school incorporates a nineteenth-century farmhouse into its modern main structure. This awareness of the "old and the new" also appears with regard to the pupil population. In reporting on a recent Board of Education meeting, for example, the *Parma Dispatch,* a local newspaper, quoted the following from a statement by the President of the Board;

Parma School's behavior problems seem to be no more severe than what could be expected in a rapidly growing system. The system is feeling the effects of the few people who have moved in bringing their problems with them. . . . The number of student suspensions is up in the system, but so is enrollment. Only a few of the suspensions are permanent.

Parma is new, growing, burgeoning, and it is very aware of this newness. On the other hand, it likes to believe that there are roots. This constant awareness of the need for coping with the new, combined with a concern for tradition and propriety, encourages the ambivalence typifying Parma. Many of its students are transfers and judge Parma in terms of what they have known before,

> I think the best thing that ever happened to me in Parma was basically just going and enjoying this school very much. Please don't get me wrong. I'm not saying this to win over whoever is correcting this test. I really enjoy going to this school.[1]

The contrary opinion was voiced by another student,

> The worst thing that ever happened to me in High School was going to this school. Out of all the schools I've been to this is by far the worst. Their is no freedom whatsoever. A student has no identity. Its like a giant factory turning out the same old line every June.

A paternalistic concern, in deference to what ought to be, characterizes the image Parma seeks to project about itself. The student handbook, through which the school authority speaks to its students, contains thirty-two carefully numbered general rules. Of these, the following are a representative sample,

> (4) Fighting or unnecessary roughness to the extent that anyone is liable to injury is forbidden.
> (9) The performance of any acts of conduct that interfere with the best interests of the school is forbidden.
> (12) No student is allowed to remain in the school building after school hours without being under a teacher's supervision.

Four of the thirty-two specifically refer to behavior in the school corridors. Of these, two short rules summarize the spirit of the law,

> (22) Absolutely no running or pushing in the halls, classrooms, etc.

[1] In the written responses to the Best Thing-Worst Thing Test, grammar, spelling, and punctuation are the students', not the authors'.

(25) No boisterous laughing or talking during assembly or in the halls.

That the student will be held accountable for his feelings and actions, as the above rules reveal in differing degrees, was supported by student reactions to the project testing. Only Parma students expressed concern about the possibility that their responses might be seen by teachers and school administrators. "Are you interviewing some of us later?" asked one young lady, and then added immediately, "Then we have to account for our answers."

A more pointed description of each school than handbooks offer is obtained through use of the ressentiment index and the Best Thing-Worst Thing Test. In the case of the index, several statements drawn from the F-N R Index will be used to characterize the school. Of course, these statements are only accurate to the degree that the respondent's perception reflects true conditions in the school and should only be accepted with some caution. To explain the process by which we chose such statements, a digression is necessary.

The selection of key items is based on a standard Chi-square test of significance. For example, Item (1) of the F-N R Index says, "Students here know that in science the easiest way to solve a problem is usually the best way." Keyed false-as-ressentiment, this item somewhat simple mindedly restates Occam's Razor and is designed to measure the extent to which high school teachers use the complexities of their subject to intimidate their students—a practice we conceive of as being ressentient. Fifty-five percent of all students answered this item as false, its keyed answer. At one extreme lies Delphi, where students answered false in 71 percent of the cases, and at the other, St. Elmo, where 39 percent answered false. Comparing these separate school responses with the grand average for all students by means of a Chi-square test, with one degree of freedom, a difference in percentage points from a mean of 55 that is greater than + 9.8 is significant at 5 percent. The difference recorded by Delphi (+ 16) is well beyond even the 1 percent level. For this test, as the grand average for all respondents increases towards 100 percent or decreases towards 0 percent the span imposed by the confidence limits narrows, and at a grand average of

75 percent (or 25 percent) a difference greater than $+ 8.5$ from the grand average is significant at the 5 percent level. Similar limits can be computed for every point along the range, and it is by means of these that a determination of the significance of each school's response can be made.

From time to time we use teachers' responses to such statements to supplement our description of the school. Given the small number of teachers participating from each school, however, we have not attempted to compute confidence limits by school, and generally report the teacher response in real numbers or as an approximation. In the case of Item (1), which we have used as an example above, 65 percent of our teachers answered the statement false. An interesting aside, though, is the response, when taken as a unit, of twelve teachers who identified themselves as either science or mathematics teachers. Of these, nine answered Item (1) as true, that is, gave the nonressentient answer. On the other hand thirty-four of the forty-five remaining teachers answered the item as false. This is certainly an impressive contrast in response.

Now, back to Parma, and to the items on which Parma scores differ significantly from those of other schools.[2] At all schools students agree that "The student newspaper . . . is pretty careful not to print anything too critical . . ." or "not to report things in such a way that they might make trouble for the school. . . ." At Parma, they are even more emphatic in affirming these positions. Parma students also maintain that "Dances are heavily chaperoned . . ." and that "Initiations . . . are carefully controlled to see that there isn't any rough stuff." Parma teachers concur in these statements, as they also do that "The school takes the position that students are too young to get too involved with one another." In terms of negatives, both students and teachers do *not* agree that the "Students . . . are left pretty well to themselves to do what seems reasonable to them in their clubs and activities," or that "The good teachers . . . wouldn't expect a student to tell on a friend who he knows is breaking the rules." [3]

[2] Data for all items included in the F-N R Index are presented in Appendix A, Part I, including identification of significant items when tested by the Chi-square procedure described above.

[3] Items (2), (18), (48), (50), (16), (4), and (19) in Appendix A,

Two items, among several, provide an interesting contrast between students and teachers. Parma teachers maintain by a vote of six to one that "To be an honor student" at Parma means that the pupil "really knows a lot about the subjects" he's taken. The students are less sanguine about the possibility. Forty percent of them think that this is not true of Parma honor students. On the other hand, the students maintain that they "can wear anything" they want to at school "as long as it is decent." Here, the teachers disagree. They should, too, for there are dress regulations at Parma, regulations which the students saw fit to deny existed. On one final item, agreement was general and appropriate: both teachers and students held that "When it is really hot" Parma's basketball team "is a beautiful thing to watch." It was, too, and combining excellence with efficiency was the district champion during the season the project was on location.[4]

Parma students, in describing their school environment through the medium of the ressentiment index, rated their school an unex-

Table 1. Mean Ressentiment Scores of the Nine Schools (Phase I)[5]

School	Mean R Score	Standard Deviation
Martingale	69.6	± 8.6
Milgrim	69.2	± 9.3
Parma	63.1	± 9.2
Hartsburgh	63.1	± 10.9
Caddo	63.0	± 9.4
St. Elmo	61.2	± 9.5
Delphi	58.0	± 9.6
Havencrest	56.9	± 11.3
Ipswich	56.2	± 9.3

Part I. Throughout this book, when several items are grouped together for descriptive purposes, item numbers in Appendix A, Part I, will be specified in a footnote so that the reader can ascertain the source of the statement.

[4] Items (53), (12), and (22).

[5] See Appendix A, Part II, for discussion of these scores.

ceptional 63.1, near the average for all schools (See Table 1). This places Parma in the middle group of schools, along with Hartsburgh, Caddo, and St. Elmo, and in itself is not especially informative. The item-by-item analysis, on the other hand, is much richer both in details and in its substantive implications. In sum, Parma students support, through their item responses to the F-N R Index, a description of their school as an institution bent on exercising paternalistic control over both feelings and actions. Generally, the teachers concur. The pattern, however, becomes more complex when we turn to the responses from the Best Thing-Worst Thing Test.

Jean Walker, for instance, in describing her Best Thing, mentioned a teacher,

> Not only does he excel in his field of teaching . . . but each child, student or hood is considered by him to be equal no matter what his reputation may have been beforehand. Foolish teenage problems are treated with utmost care.

Jean's Worst Thing was about classroom experience,

> The day I became excellerated . . . I began to resent the quiet inner rage inside of me errupting every time I was called "stupid" or didn't answer a question. I hated it and still do.

It is not clear what Jean hated, the experience or herself; nor is it clear what she should have hated. But she seems to have preferred ressentiment to classroom pressure.

Fifteen percent of Parma's students mentioned positive peer group associations in their Best Thing, responding with variations of,

> The best thing is when I moved here and made good friends quickly. I got into the right group and met the right girls. I got accepted very quickly and am making out good.

On the other hand, 13 percent expressed disillusionment with their peers as the Worst Thing. This category ranked second among Worst Things at Parma after "failing a subject" (16 percent). Along with Jean Walker's previously cited askant comment "hood," we have,

Nothing really bad has ever happened to *me* while I have been at Parma. Perhaps the event that gave me the worst feeling was one that occurred this past year. One of Parma's top students, a very pretty, popular girl, got into "trouble." Until this time many of my friends and I held her in great esteem; in fact almost to the point of idolization. My faith in the student body of Parma was a little shaken after this news to say the least. This event made me see only more clearly the bad points of our community and to realize the need of certain changes.

Somehow, the meaning of "Worst" has been confounded.

Legitimate authority at Parma seeks to be understanding, and people who are in charge try to be helpful,

> The best thing was the day I passed a French exam. I was so pleased I framed the test. My teacher was very proud of me. He only wishes I could pass some more.

It isn't always as clear, however, that the person counts, not just his grades, but it is clear that there is a Parma way to act, and that this is where the sympathy comes in. Consider, for instance, this comment by Donald Jones,

> I think the worst thing was that I was forced to shave off my goatee. I was told by the vice-principal that there was no rule concerning anything like this, yet I was told to shave it off or get out. I think the administration is very narrow-minded about some things around here. I could not see where my growing a goatee was affecting students to the point where they could not keep up with their work.

The Parma Way is compelling and controlling, coupled with a certain solicitude. There is much about this way that seems to leave the student feeling small and confused. Its pressure confounds, and it is difficult to determine where one belongs—whether inside, submitting, or outside, in revolt. Claudia described her worst experience most concretely,

> Last year, when my boy friend and I were holding hands in the hall. I could see nothing shameful about this. I am a good girl and my boy friend and I have been going steady for almost

ten months. At the time we were going steady only a few days. A teacher came up and told us to break it up. We did, but my boy friend turned around and said "thanks" very nastily, which was the wrong thing to do but anyway they got into an argument and then a fight and pretty soon my boyfriend got kicked out of school. I was very scared, it was in the paper, but luckily my name wasn't. It just said a girl. But my father is very strict and I knew if he ever found out that would be the end of me, you see, he belongs to the PTA and all. In other schools very near students *can* hold hands without being prosecuted for it. I think kissing and other things *are* way out of line for school, *but not just holding hands.*

Against this there are other aspects to the Parma way of life,

The best thing that ever happened to me in high school was joining the football team. You are respected.

Obviously, something doesn't jibe at Parma. There is a formal concern for order, especially for orderly feelings; and most of the students are contrite in the face of that concern. They have come to accept in passive acquiescence the limitations imposed there on adolescent expression. But often their stand is awkward, their responses incongruous and unresolved, as if they can't quite express themselves. Confusion seems to be the price of Parma's ambivalent mood.

One thing is certain, however: the press imposed at Parma does not make it a comfortable place to be. Possibly, it isn't supposed to be, for this may be the way education is conceived of there. At Parma one "must learn to grow up" it would seem, even though it hurts. Nevertheless, and in keeping with Parma's characterizing ambivalence, Jimmy O'Brien unexpectedly did find comfort there one day, and described it as his Best Thing,

I think the best thing that ever happened to me was last year during final examinations. I know it's a funny time to have a good thing happen but I seem to remember having an awfully good time. You had to stay in school even if you didn't have tests. But the thing was, you had the run of the school if you didn't have review classes—complete freedom of movement.

Nothing particular happened to me. I just had the best time in school that I'd ever had.

HARTSBURGH HIGH SCHOOL

Some people think our students are apathetic. . . .
A Guidance Counselor

Model adolescents on the whole, our Hartsburgh respondents profess especially to like being what they ought to be. They like each other, their teachers, and the subject matter they are studying, or so they said,

> The best thing was the introduction, through classes, of the vast fields of knowledge and learning available. The history of literature and backgrounds in science, math and foreign languages are the most stimulating things I have met in high school.

They also like achievement, appreciate receiving academic medals, making the Honor Roll, and "getting something out of school." For instance, one young candidate, Jack Armstrong, described himself,

> I am an active member of the traffic squad, one of the four Lieutenants. Being on the squad has done a great deal to mold my future convictions and morals. I have been put in the position as to judge which will I hold in greater stead—my friends or my morals and principles. It has made me a great deal more mature and rational than I would have been.

Presumption suggests that our Jack is no budding E. M. Forster, and that he will resolve his dilemma in favor of his morals and principles. They try, these young people of Hartsburgh, to live according to the established model, and they should make good members of someone's Establishment.

> The best thing that ever happened to me was when I began to understand why I am here. I started seeing the teacher's point of view which for years I had always been against. I also began to realize the true meaning of life.

The same theme appears again, in obverse image, in the Worst Thing responses. The pupil lives under scrutiny at Hartsburgh and with constant judgment as a companion. He must be careful of his reputation; "a bad Rep" can hurt,

> The worst thing was starting off on the wrong foot in this school. I didn't give myself a very good name with my teachers and there's no way of showing them or making up for it now.

Once it has caught on, a bad Rep doesn't get lost easily,

> The only thing I can think of that was "bad" is the time during assembly when my friend accidently let slip a "cuss word" in front of the whole school, and we were connected with the mishap for the next few months.

In consequence, the sensible student at Hartsburgh learns to be careful, to conserve his capital,

> The worst thing that ever happened to me in high school was getting caught loaning my car to "friends" to cut school with. It wasn't just the part about getting caught that was bad but just that I was stupid enough to want to do somebody a favor and have it spoil your chances in school for such things as Honor Society, etc.

And to accept his own limitations,

> The worst thing was taking subjects I really didn't like, just to make my parents happy. When my marks went down I got into all kinds of trouble at home and school became a terrible experience.

The impression is one of a hard life of duty. For escape, some try fantasy. For example, Duncan Robot's response to the Non-Verbal Perception Test was the most elaborate and different one returned from any school. In its own way it is an articulate statement about the institutional climate at Hartsburgh. This task, it will be remembered, asked the respondent to draw and describe an ideal social studies classroom. The Figure shows Duncan's response, together with his detailed instructions.

Imagine that we are going to have a new high school in the community and that you have been asked to submit a design for the social studies classroom that you will spend most of your time in. In the space below roughly sketch this ideal classroom—please be sure to label all the important areas and details.

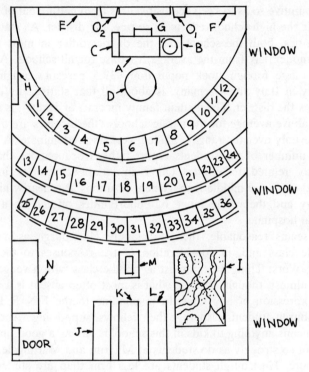

Legend:
A   Teaching Complex + Desk
B   Phonograph (Hi-fi Stereo)
C   Electronic Control Complex*
D   "Mammoth" Globe
E, F, & H Maps
G   Screen for slides, movies
I   War Strategy Table
J, K, & L Book and Record Library

M   Projection Table
N   Storage
O_1 Regular Television (Color)
O_2 Closed Circuit Television
1–12   Student Desks
13–24   Pupil Desks
25–36   Visitor or Observer Desks

*The electronic control complex controls B, D, E, F, G, H, M, O_1, O_2, and locks and unlocks the door, contains a clock which is visible only to the teacher (to keep students, pupils, etc. from gazing at the clock) and can also deliver a 10 volt jolt to anyone of the desks 13–36 and a 5 volt jolt to desks 1–12, when there is an unnecessary outbreak of emotions. It also controls temperature, humidity, and amount and type of light. I have also crossed out windows and added air conditioning, to keep students, pupils, etc. from gazing out of the windows. Furniture must be very comfortable, but the room kept at a temp. level so as to keep students, pupils, etc. mentally alert. There are no black boards (to relieve chalk dust); notes are projected. This plan also creates a competitive atmosphere for seats 1–12.

Figure. Response to the Non-Verbal Perception Test by Duncan Robot of Hartsburgh.

Hartsburgh High seems somehow to have succeeded in reproducing a conventional Establishment-oriented outlook. Respectful of the symbols of achievement in its community and encouraging a mild form of upward mobility, it is at the same time sufficiently intrapunitive so as to keep acquisitiveness from getting out of hand. In this the high school reflects its source, the district. As statistical categories, both the school and the district differ in most things only moderately from the average response for all schools. A relatively large foreign stock population (39.5 percent), originating mainly in Italy and Germany, is about all that statistically distinguishes the district. The median family income, at $6,894, is somewhat above average for the public schools (the incomes are distributed evenly over the range). Skilled workers predominate. A fairly large number of the students report father's occupations that are directly related to selling. Other important categories include skilled craft and middle management positions at a nearby aircraft factory and the whole range of opportunities offered by a state mental hospital.

It seems reasonable, then, to classify Hartsburgh as middle-middle class and, in consideration of the responses to the Best Thing-Worst Thing Test, almost as middle class with a vengeance. Only almost, though, because what is most often absent is a vigorous expression of any kind. In responding to the F-N R Index, Hartsburgh students disparage their fellows, supporting "About all that means anything to kids in this school is having a good time"— but not so strongly as do students at Milgrim and Martingale. Furthermore, Hartsburgh students are less firm than are students at other high schools in the conviction that "A basic principle of the way this school is supposed to be run is that everybody gets equal treatment no matter who he is." And finally, they like the statement, "Teachers are too soft, too easy with the students here. They don't expect enough from them and don't make them work hard enough"; but still they feel this only moderately. And on most of these items the Hartsburgh teachers disagree.[6]

Subornation in reverse—that is, toward propriety—is the method of authority at Hartsburgh. While dress regulations exist they do not seem to be rigorously enforced. Instead, the students

[6] Items (30), (56), and (55).

are encouraged to do right. Every Wednesday is dress-up day; boys are expected to wear ties and jackets; the girls, dresses rather than skirts and sweaters. On Wednesday school ends with an extra hour of required assembly, and, the students explain, there are often outside visitors for whom they are expected to look their best. There is technique in this, and in the way the smoking problem is being handled. Recently, the principal issued to all students a letter warning that any student caught in the vicinity of the school with "tobacco products" on him would be subject to suspension; students were directed to have their parents sign the letter as written acknowledgment that they were aware of the regulation and then to return it to the school.

Indications suggest, however, that this is changing. Hartsburgh is a relatively new school and is still engaged in establishing itself as an institution. During its short history considerable use has been made of the self-disciplining potential of the students themselves. A Citizenship Corps—concerned, it was explained, with making the school a better place—has been charged with "law" enforcement, and each morning, during the first period, two officers of the Corps, who are students, of course, go quietly from classroom to classroom with a list, handing out summonses. In the past, such infractions as were reported were generally brought before Student Court and tried there. While this procedure still exists, a new and more formidable one has recently been instituted. An assistant principal has been appointed and charged with enforcing discipline. This has been done, according to our information, to give the newly appointed assistant principal, formerly an excellent teacher, an opportunity to learn how to be a principal and thereby a chance eventually to earn a promotion. Whatever the reasons for his appointment, the new assistant principal is now taking over many of the problems previously assigned to the Student Court, especially those reported by the teachers. In consequence, a Parkinson's Law of malefaction is having its inevitable effect. It seems that with the increased bureaucracy and the greater interest in enforcement all around, the students are being caught more often.

There is a kind of automated consistency at Hartsburgh. The students there do not express hostile feelings, but they are also not apathetic. They are concerned about success. In that sense the

subornation technique has been entirely successful; for, at Hartsburgh, the students want to do what they have been taught they
ought to do,

> I like to do as well as possible since I plan to go to college. I
> do not like to do poorly on tests and I think this is one of the
> most unpleasant things which could occur.

The evidence examined so far suggests that at Parma the student
respondents felt a kind of loss, that they were worried and often
confused, as they submitted to growing up. At Hartsburgh they are
more accepting, more willing to fit themselves in. They have come
to terms with their predicament and have learned that the only sensible thing for them to do is to make the most of it. It is, after all,
an orderly future they are preparing for, and even, in a way, one
that will be rewarding. There is a kind of practical wisdom to be
gained in school, and Hartsburgh students actively seek it. As Judy
Park wrote of her Best Thing,

> During my years in high school I have had the opportunity to
> learn what I am looking for in the future. I have never been
> Queen of the Prom or president of a Club but the experiences
> I have received and the knowledge I have gained are far more
> important.

At Hartsburgh, it seems, she has learned how to live with alienation without too much regret.

Chapter IV

THREE FORMS
OF CULTURAL
DEPRIVATION

MILGRIM HIGH SCHOOL

*A typical American community of some 50,000 popula-
tion, close to national averages in the kind of people who
live there, and in their incomes and other social characteristics. Between 1960 and 1962, the percentage of gradu-
ates going on to further schooling rose from 27 percent to
53 percent. The number of job seekers unemployed at
graduation dropped from 18 percent to 6 percent. Dropouts were reduced from 6 percent to 2 percent, and, in
1962, some of those who had dropped out were coming
back, or were enrolling in vocational schools.*

THIS DESCRIPTION of Milgrim is taken from a brochure attached
to a recent film sponsored by the U. S. Office of Education. Such
achievement is certainly creditable and suggests a forward-looking
institution endowed with energetic leadership and dedicated to fur-
thering the advance of the young people charged to its care. There
is current, however, another view of Milgrim. In his response to the
Best Thing-Worst Thing Test, a student wrote,

The worst thing that ever happened to me in this place was the
day I enrolled in here! I hate it here!

And a passing conversation with a teacher,

We're just a suburban slum.

The contrast between the image in the brochure and these comments is striking, even shocking, and immediately one must question whether these comments are not simply the obloquy of isolated malcontents. Supporting evidence, though, suggests quite the opposite and argues instead that malcontentedness is a signal feature of life at Milgrim. Something there encourages high dudgeon, overt hostility, and often oppressive authority.

With respect to student freedom Milgrim is the most punitive school studied. Fully 14 pages of Milgrim's 48-page student handbook are concerned with correct behavior, representing almost three times the attention given this subject in any of the other handbooks. Yet Milgrim seems to have intended quite the opposite, as the following from the handbook preamble suggests,

> We should all like to see the number of rules kept at a minimum. Individual self-discipline on the part of each student is the only way to accomplish this. It is based on understanding and observing the code of behavior developed for the good of all.

Regulations, including provisions governing boy-girl relations, lavatory limitations, and a warning regarding "surprise" inspections of student lockers follow. This, for example, on boy-girl relations,

> Upon entering the high school the student will find himself faced with many new and bewildering problems. Among the most important of these is dating. For many, dating has already begun in junior high; for others, the parties and dances are a completely new experience. For all, the new found freedoms of cars and parties without chaperones or "musical chairs" seem vague in the limitations they impose.
>
> For the pupil to find his place in this social whirl, he must first decide what his purpose is in high school. If he realizes that it is to obtain an education, he will regulate his social life accordingly, if not, he will find his classes difficult, if not impossible.
>
> Whether or not to go steady is a matter of perennial concern:

if not among the students, then most certainly among the parents. The one prime consideration which should guide you is that you are responsible for your actions; that they also reflect on your parents and school. An indiscretion on your part, even such a simple thing as holding hands in the hall, can be misconstrued as a mark of improper training. In simple words, this means: don't broadcast your affections all over the walls of the school; because, by the time the ink dries on "John loves Mary," John probably loves Ella, and Mary is headover heels in love with Tom.

As for "smooching" in the halls, doorways, classrooms, corners, lockers, lunchrooms: Don't. It gives your parents and the school a bad name, besides smearing the girl's lipstick.

Keeping these things in mind the four years of high school will provide healthy and normal development, not only physically and mentally, but also emotionally.

If there is any misconduct on the school grounds or disobeying of the school regulations the student may be tried by the Student Court.[1] If for any reasons he is not tried by the court, he will be referred to the Principal's office. All disciplinary action becomes a part of the student's permanent record, with the exception of student court cases. These records are often requested by employers and colleges.

As might be expected, Milgrim scores significantly high on Item (16) of the F-N *R* Index. The item reads, "The school takes the position that students are too young to get too involved with one another." The teachers disagree.

Lavatories are a special focus of concern at Milgrim. Here, the only time these facilities may be used is during class time. All washrooms are locked during the four-minute recess between class periods. When the bell rings for the period to begin, a custodian methodically unlocks all the washroom doors. As a result a pass, issued by the classroom instructor, is necessary for each occasion

---

[1] According to student respondents there is no longer a Student Court at Milgrim. We were told that the "hoody element" had gained control and were dismissing charges against most of the defendants, usually their close friends, either through acquittal or by accepting pleas of insanity.

of use. "Why," we inquired of one young man, "are the washrooms locked between classes?" "Too much smoking," was his prompt reply. One further item on washrooms: only 14 of the 902 Phase I subjects included lavatories as part of their classroom design for the Non-Verbal Perception Test. Six of these were students at Milgrim—reflecting, it would seem, a felt need.

The ressentiment index gives further evidence of the censorious spirit that saturates Milgrim. The overall score places Milgrim second highest at 69.2, only half a point below Martingale. When scores for all teachers are considered alone, Milgrim's teachers score highest in ressentiment. The same is true of female students at Milgrim. Here, the girls score almost as high as the boys. Where, on the grand average, there is a three-point spread between boys and girls scores, at Milgrim the spread is less than one point.

Such high scores imply that Milgrim is highly ressentient, an impression with which we are not entirely comfortable. It is not that the school may not want to be ressentient, for the extensive quotation on boy-girl relations suggests that it does. Rather, it is that we have always tended to view ressentient hostility as secretive, whereas at Milgrim the pattern is consistently forthright, as well as harsh.

Among the statements on which Milgrim scores significantly high in terms of keyed ressentiment are "A Student who gets on anybody's black list . . . has a pretty hard time; it practically takes a lawyer to get him off" and "If a teacher or administrator accuses a student of misbehavior . . . , there isn't much he can do to defend himself." While the teachers disagree on these two, they do agree with the students that "Students here often feel like they are butting their heads against a stone wall." [2]

The teachers disagreed on two other statements favored by Milgrim students. Both statements refer snidely to a corruption of the teaching function: "The way to get good marks . . . is to tell the teachers what they want to hear" and "Playing up to teachers and getting on their good side is the smart thing to do around here." [3] These are only a few of the items on which Milgrim scores significantly, chosen to indicate that student subjects there see their

[2] Items (42), (52), and (25).
[3] Items (5) and (43).

school as an alien, even hostile force which must be dealt with almost, it would seem, as if it were an enemy. Their interpretation is not altogether mistaken, either. Success comes hard at Milgrim, harder than at any of the other schools. Students at Milgrim reported the lowest grade average of any school—76.7 percent. By comparison, most of the school sample groups averaged around 80 percent.

Responses to the Best Thing-Worst Thing Test support these observations and to some degree explain them. Jim Gara commented, in his Worst Thing,

> I got caught smoking in school. If they had a smoking place for us no one would have to sneak. Most of the kids mothers and fathers let them smoke so why not the school. The school don't know what there talking about most of the time. Most of the teachers send you down the office and then make the offence that you did worst then what it really is. As much as I dislike the school I still need school and I like the kids. So I guess its not really to bad.

And Jean Thompson had this to say,

> The worst thing was my being caught smoking in the girls-room. I have permission to smoke, but I don't appreciate it being on my card permanently.

In an entirely different context, Micky Marello reports that her Worst Thing was,

> The time I got suspended for one day just because a teacher think my dress was too short, but it wasn't.

The "but it wasn't" is important. It is difficult to believe that a Hartsburgh student would ever make such a statement, and while a Parma student might, she would probably catch herself, deny she had said it, and twist it all out of shape. Not at Milgrim, though. Unlike the other schools described, these young people stick to their guns and stick together. When they write or talk they bring a different set of values into the discussion; and they measure their school experience against that alien set of values.

Yet, there is a worry that runs as a constant theme through Milgrim responses—the fear of the Record. Unlike Hartsburgh, with its Rep, which is something one carries in his very being, the record is an artifact, with an independent existence. It is also a potential danger. Remember Jean Thompson, the young lady endangered by being caught smoking—she didn't want it on her card. There are others,

> I guess nothing has happened to me because I won't let myself get into trouble because I want a clean record here.

And,

> The worst thing was when I got sent to the office for fighting with this boy who broke my ring. It may sound childish but I was so scared. I was sent to the office and they gave me three days detention. My mother was mad and it was just a horrible experience talking to the principal and the detention went on my record for that year.

At Milgrim to keep out of trouble is to keep your card clean, and with a little luck, one often succeeds. A year completed with a clean record represents progress and is about all that the run-of-the-mill Milgrim student hopes for,

> Nothing good happens here because things are so dull and boring. You just do your work and pass or else stay another year.

In socioeconomic terms Milgrim stands somewhat lower than Hartsburgh, yet on the whole it represents comfort rather than deprivation. Nevertheless the evidence describing the institutional press at the school suggests a way of life rich in negative affect and steeped in conflict. On the one hand, there is a clear line of authority in the hands of the educators, authority that is enforced and carries with it, in its ominous Record, severe sanctions. On the other hand, there is a student body at Milgrim that is not particularly strong in academic competence but that is most independent in its spirit. As previously indicated there are two sets of values operating at Milgrim—the set imposed by the school and that of the students. The school's values are incorporated in its technique and represent the greater world of education and success; those of the students emerge from the community out of which they come —the so-called suburban slum.

Data on the number of persons per room at home suggest that Milgrim students come from homes that are more crowded than is conventional for suburbia. While comfortable, these are not wealthy people; in professional and managerial occupations, Milgrim hardly exceeds the much poorer Caddo district. In substance, Milgrim is a blue-collar town; its workers are assemblers, truck drivers, meatcutters, and exterminators. They work with their hands. Work is important to them, and a part of their needs pattern. One of the R index items on which both Milgrim and Martingale agreed, was Item (11), "The best thing about courses in shop and homemaking is that they teach you how to enjoy working with your hands."

Milgrim's young people attend a school that has high aspirations for them—a modern, progress-oriented, college-focused school. And they attend as the children of blue-collar workers. Here, it seems, is located the root cause of the conflict. As one young lady observed,

> Nothing drastic or bad ever happened to me in school. I never got caught doing anything. I have had only one detention in 3 years and got caught smoking once. They threaten you with death and destruction and its really very childish. They want everyone to stay young and then graduate and get hit with life all at once.

Milgrim, known nationally as a "good" school, is in many ways a "tough" school. Nevertheless, it misses in its impact on its students. The reason for this paradox, however, is not that the school isn't trying to do well by its students, but rather, that it cannot in the present context. The values of the school are simply not at one with those of the community. Or, what was Worst was,

> Not understanding when I first came the other people, or my role. Feeling as if you don't like this type of society and would rather be someplace else.

MARTINGALE HIGH SCHOOL

If you're average—I feel that you're not better than anyone else, you're equal among both of them . . . you're equal to the better and you're equal to the worst.

A Martingale Student

Central to any understanding of Martingale is an awareness of the unique socioeconomic pattern of the school district. Begun a number of years ago as an integrated housing development, the Martingale community is now a suburban hamlet of some 7,000 persons, favored by few of the advantages of suburban living and afflicted with most of its problems. The school itself is new but small, the smallest public school studied, and the district is poor. Lacking a library, theater, or even an ice-cream parlor, the hamlet has few facilities for its youth. Also, lacking prosperous commercial properties, it has an inadequate tax base with which to support its schools. As a result, teacher salaries at Martingale average between two to five hundred dollars below those of the surrounding communities. For this reason teachers do not stay long, and less than 25 percent of the instructional staff has tenure.

At the present time some 60 percent of Martingale's residents are Negro, with this percentage growing. Another 20 percent are of foreign stock. Their houses are small, snug, and well kept. Several have swimming pools. Surrounded by open fields Martingale is often described as rural. This cozy appearance is deceptive, however, for, unlike its neighbors, Martingale is not progressing. Very few persons are moving in and building there. Its open land is not a sign of prosperity; it is, instead, a measure of its isolation from the expanding suburbia which surrounds it. Quite simply, Martingale is a pariah town; it doesn't belong.

When measured by median family income Martingale is not the poorest of the schools studied—Caddo is, with Martingale a close second at $5,854. But by almost every other measure—occupation, education, or utilization of housing—Martingale ranks at the bottom. Many Martingale adults are employed in state hospitals in the neighborhood. Others work for small businesses—gas stations, contractors, and fuel-oil vendors. Often mothers work as well as fathers, and the children must care for themselves. The lot is not easy for Martingale's people.

Martingale is the one school studied that has, on the basis of census figures, a serious dropout problem. Cultural deprivation, depressed goals, and the many parentless and one-parent homes all suggest reasons for this poor performance. Moreover, as Martingale teachers take care to point out, Martingale students, when tested for intelligence, rank average or below average in ability. In planning coursework for such students, the school accepts this finding that many of its students are scholastically slow and adjusts the process to this slowness. This it does even as it rejects the implication that the slowness necessarily implies stupidity. If it is to work, such conscious adjustment certainly demands highly skilled and expensive teaching, but this is exactly the kind Martingale does not have the means to support. As a result, Martingale students rarely have an opportunity to experience academic fulfillment in school.

In sum then, an underpaid staff, poor social facilities, poverty, and low academic performance in a suburban ghetto all cooperate to perpetuate a situation fraught with low morale. Martingale is a deprived area where people properly might feel deprived. Do the young people there, and, if so, how do they express this feeling?

To begin with, Martingale students agree with the above estimate. They don't really want to be where they are. Their most popular Best Thing is field trips,

> I think the best thing that ever happen to me was when I went with my history club to Washington, D.C. It was very exciting and I could do it all over again.

Field trips, of course, are an adventure outside, a movement away. Martingale is the only school in which this category emerges *at all* on the Best Thing-Worst Thing Test.

At 69.6 Martingale also scores highest for all schools on the ressentiment index. Here, choices on many items paralleled those of Milgrim, and focusing on these items as a unit is particularly instructive. There are fourteen such items on the F-N R Index and seventeen on the Stern R Index. Together, these items contribute over two thirds of Martingale's range above the average for all schools. When their effect is subtracted from the Martingale score, the net result in terms of scores makes Martingale similar to Parma or St. Elmo. These items affect the Milgrim score in a similar manner.[4]

Taken together, the fourteen R items roughly describe a vulgarization of the educational process. Outstanding among them, for instance, is Item (15), "The teachers who have a good line, who know the latest jokes, and who always manage to make the class hour a lot of fun are the ones the students here like best." Two others denigrate teaching and learning, "What students here like about biology is that a lot of good off-color jokes can be told in class without anyone being the wiser" and "Students here know that poetry is supposed to be beautiful but deep down they also know that the biggest part of it is pure bunk." The two "cheating" items are also included; respondents disagree that "Most students here are too proud to cheat on examinations" and agree that "When they don't know the answers and you do, the other students here expect you to help them, such as, when taking a test, by giving them a chance to see your paper." In other words, the intention is to make education into something that is fun, and if that is impossible, then into something that the student can, with the help of his fellows, handle.[5]

The same elements recur in the items from the Stern R Index, with a special note of bitterness and estrangement added. Paraphrasing several, we find the students describing the teaching in their schools as indifferent when not either silly or actively hostile, punishments that are arbitrary, and a school that is engaged in infantilizing its students. Altogether, the R index responses paint a thoroughly disagreeable picture of a minor-key class struggle. The young people know that they are in enemy territory and take appropriate defensive measures. They work at encouraging their mentors to vulgarize education so that they can live with it.

[4] The items for the F-N R Index are (3), (8), (9), (11), (15), (17), (27), (29), (30), (31), (41), (55), (63), and 73. An analysis of their effect is developed more completely in terms of a dependency factor analysis in The Project Report, CRP 1758 (New York: Brooklyn College, 1965), pp. 54-57.

[5] Items (9), (41), (63), and (3).

There is an important difference between Martingale and Milgrim, however. While both describe an alien system that sets standards they must live up to, the Martingale students, although realistic about those standards and their implications, are not necessarily against the school. For, in Martingale, education has an instrumental value; it can lead to a different way of life. And they want that.

The difference is most clearly expressed through the Best Thing-Worst Thing Test. At Martingale the students are most concrete; they talk about the things and the people they like and don't like,

> My best thing was when I started taking my art course in the ninth grade I found out I really could draw. I received a sewing machine, and I can really wear the clothes I make, so maybe I wan't just dreaming after all I may become a fashion designer.

They are also practical in their aspirations, and it is through these that they accept the institution, when it can help them make something of themselves. Gloria wrote,

> The best thing is the time I got on the Honor Roll. It made me feel very proud and my parents also. I will try as hard as I can to keep up my work and try to get to be a Navy Nurse.

They are not consistent, however, when they eschew poetry, for they are often expressively poetic. They seem to be able to afford sentimentality and to combine it with a quiet dignity. Phoenicia Scott wrote that her Best Thing was,

> When I met a boy name Robert, my husband to be in August. And also when I am almost on my own. I think being 18, is the best thing can happen to a teenager. Having responsibility of your own with loving parents.

Many Martingale students express a certain inner harmony which must be reckoned with when considering the institutional press established by the school. In their positive mode they come to terms with averageness. One thoughtful young man, during his Phase II interview, pointed out that he himself was average, and that what he was interested in was the average person. Affirming that he liked his own life with no one telling him what to do, he made a virtue of being average; that, being all that he expected, had become what he wanted. But unlike the students at Hartsburgh, who have a similar philosophy, they are not unctuous about averageness at Martingale; they earnestly believe in it. Moreover, the school, supporting as it does through its promotions and certifications an average-accessible form of competence, has something worthwhile to offer these young people. And they respect it for what it is.

Negative Martingale responses are direct and personal. They single out individuals to dislike rather than processes to complain about,

> The worst thing is being in Mr. Long's class. All he is is a conceited teacher. He thinks everyone should love him. I know I'm not good in his subject but he doesn't have to make me feel 1 inch high when he gets through talking to me.

And, again,

> The worst thing that happened to me was being put in Carlson's class. That woman has got to go! Last year she failed me with a 45. Now again this year I have the bitch and leave it to her and I guess I'll fail again.

In their responses Martingale students describe a system with which they have made a certain peace. They are outwardly mobile if not upwardly mobile, and for them the school is a means of access to a greater world. As a result, they are not as hostile toward their school as are Milgrim's students, even though they utilize many of the same ressentiment items in describing it. When they are unhappy they don't single out the school for blame; instead they castigate specific individuals. They accept the school as being all it can be.

This mode of accomodation distorts the press at Martingale. The pose is defensive as well as hopefully constructive and encourages acceptance of the system, with all its apparent limitations. It is true that Martingale students are often incompetent. But are they also slow? It is not clear, although they are quite convincing in declaring themselves to be slow. This is a way the defensive pose is expressed. Yet, along side this pose is a certain directness, a sensible attention to matters at hand, and a kind of shrewdness such as one associates with peasants. As a result, the press, which tries to make them what they probably want to be, and also probably cannot be, escapes them, loses them, or washes off. It just isn't felt the way it is at Milgrim.

CADDO HIGH

The best thing that ever happened was when I played my first Football game and made the guy playing opposite me know he wasn't messing with just a nothing.

A Caddo Student

Caddo is different. More than 50 percent of our respondents from the nine schools reported that they "often feel like they are butting their heads against a stone wall." At Milgrim the feeling was especially popular whereas at Caddo it is *not*. Almost 60 percent of the 902 student subjects in our entire sample reported that they thought that their "good teachers [would] . . . expect a student to tell on a friend who [they knew was] . . . breaking the rules." Parma students were very firm in this conviction while Caddo students disagreed. Caddo is also described by its students as a place where "The main thing that keeps initiations from getting too rough . . . is that the members and pledges really like one another. . . ." [6]

These items drawn from the F-N R Index indicate that at Caddo students do not feel harassed or driven. Otherwise, Caddo's response to the index was unexceptional; the mean score for student respondents there, 63.0, is close to the mean for all schools, 62.4. Caddo also generates fewer significant ressentiment items than does any other school. The teacher respondents, however, differ with the students about this; they rate Caddo above average in ressentiment (63.1, as against 56.1 for teachers from all schools).

[6] Items (25), (19), and (6).

Incidentally, they also place their school a tenth of a point higher than do the students.

Located at the outer margin of suburbia, Caddo is almost rural in character. While Caddo's median income, $5,830, is the lowest for all public schools, poverty does not seem to be an important element in Caddo life. Caddo's parents are primarily factory workers. Many of them are employed as machinists or assemblers in nearby airplane factories. Caddo's working mothers, and many are, are classified as semiskilled rather than unskilled. Only half as many Caddo men and women work as service workers or laborers as do Martingale parents. Thus, while in little danger of making a fortune, Caddo's parents are employed in stable, respected occupations. As with Milgrim's parents, they are blue-collar people.

It is a canon of local mythology that Caddo has a very large foreign population, composed mainly of persons of Italian and Slavic extraction. Supposedly, these people are culturally conditioned to accept a working-class way of life. As they are not overly concerned with improving themselves, it is alleged, they can take success-striving or leave it. To them and their progeny is attributed the relative peace and calm at Caddo. However, neither the census data nor a name check of the students in the sample support this explanation. In fact, Caddo's foreign stock composition differs little, actually, from that of Hartsburgh or Milgrim.

The high school at Caddo is an imposing structure. In explaining it one teacher said, "The community questioned our building such an expensive school—but it's good. People are poor here, and they look up to it. All the teachers are respected."

Poor or not, respectful or not, Caddo people seem to have come to terms with their circumstances and to have passed on this gift of peace to their children. It is notable that there is little evidence of poverty in the student responses. Their economic circumstances hardly seem to interfere with their activities, possibly because their activities are consonant with their poverty. Their immediate concerns are their serious concerns, and they follow through with them.

Report cards, for example, are important to students at Caddo. They appear often among the things both Best and Worst. Charlie Horton made his Best Thing point in this way,

Report	English	92	Drawing	95	Days Absent	0
Card:	Math	96	Gym	95	Days Tardy	0
	Geography	91				

And for Rachel Finch, her Worst Thing was,

When I found out that I failed Algebra for the 3rd time.

In these responses, Caddo students contrast sharply with those at Hartsburgh. At Hartsburgh both acceptance within the system and creditable progress towards one's future were of vital importance. The identity, the Rep, became an artifact to be sustained, and a certain pretension infected the students' statements about their best and worst experiences. At Caddo, on the other hand, grades, a relative judgment by the system, are taken at their face value. The student either likes or hates, and says so. Grades are a part of reality, not an obsession. He doesn't let himself become absorbed into them.

Yet there is more to Caddo than individuals winning small, immediate victories, or for several bitter moments, suffering defeat. There is also an artlessness that is so youthful, so unexpected. Compare for example, Caddo's Muriel Carrara with Jack Armstrong or Judy Park of Hartsburgh. Muriel wrote,

The best thing was the meeting and making of friends. This may seem to you unimportant, but not to me. These different people around me is what makes my years in high school so interesting. Each individual has something to offer: the teachers make you more intellectual with books and the students by their everyday actions.

Now this certainly sounds stuffy—everyone being such a good fellow. Is it honest, or is it just something for the outsider to be impressed with? For Caddo, yes, it seems it is honest; it is the way young people there were found to be. Liking each other was important. Consider also Kate Rogers' Worst experience,

The worst thing was that I had a big fight with my history teacher. I had asked for a pass to the girls room and when I came back I put the pass on his desk and the pass fell off and

he thought I had thrown it their. He brought me out in the hall
and he started to scream at me.

Were this Martingale, Miss Rogers would stand in danger of becoming a "marked" person; at Milgrim it would go on her Record;
at Hartsburgh, become part of her Rep; but at Caddo things are
different. Miss Rogers continued,

After that he didn't quite like me and I guess that I kind of
disliked him too. But this year I have the same teacher for
W. History and we are the best of friends. In fact I got a ninety
this year.

The faculty at Caddo doesn't seem to be very concerned about
remembering or punishing; and transfer students sometimes find
such laxity a bit disconcerting,

When I first came to this school I found out the teachers favor
students too much and some teachers let students get away
with murder and still pass them.

Others, however, feel quite differently,

Before Caddo I was attending Glendennon [a nearby school].
There all they do is have fights with another school. Then my
coming to Caddo changed my whole out-look on school. Meeting fine pupils and wonderful teachers.

Caddo "rules" are not such, exactly, but rather are rationales for
conduct that is deemed appropriate. On dress and grooming the
student handbook has the following to say,

The general appearance and grooming of people reflects
strongly on their characters and attitudes, and just as there
are styles appropriate to work and play, so too are there types
of dress and appearance considered acceptable in school.
There is considerable difficulty in specifically stating the different types of dress which are within the framework of social
propriety, so students are instructed by their teachers concerning the clothing, hair styles, etc., which are regarded in poor
taste. Certainly one of the surest ways of exhibiting self-respect

and gaining the respect of others is by displaying a neat and conservative appearance.

And, on the corridor pass, this rationale,

A pass system is used in order that a record may be kept of the location of students in the building.

Should those in authority at Caddo ever become interested in making life difficult for the young people there, such "rules" would certainly be adequate to the task. Caddo's instructions are philanthropic, are phrased in the sacred cant of dissembling administration, and seek to promote conventionality in the young through enticing their interest. Used with malice, as ressentiment, they could be made to hurt. But they don't seem to be so used at Caddo, and, in consequence, enthusiasm in its most adolescent forms continues to thrive there.

Our examination of Caddo underscores the element of context in establishing the relationship between a school press and those subject to that press. When we began this study several years ago we anticipated, somewhat naïvely, the existence of a simple dialectical model, of an institutional press constructed in terms of the intentions of the school administration and imposed on a set of students. The evidence now suggests that the situation is clearly more complex, for the press exists both as principles and as persons implementing those principles. And such persons can include teachers, counselors, fellow students, and even the secretary in the office, as well as administrators.

While specific principles may more or less facilitate ressentiment, they only serve as passive instruments. More importantly, ressentiment is manifested in the actions of those with an opportunity and a need to express it. The procedures and practices of the institution are there to be used, and their possibilities can be exploited and are, with ingenuity and variety. As used, they constitute the unique press of the institution, they give it its nature. This is what we mean by context. Such presses as there are can be overtly oppressive, confused, steeped in ressentiment, fair, or, we hope somehow, somewhere, just plain friendly.

At Milgrim, the press is fierce and contradicting. Directing its students along paths chosen by the greater society, the school there is concerned with making its students into something they are not, and it judges them and itself accordingly. The students reciprocate with the same spirit. This torment emerges as conflict within the school, and sometimes, as a gush of energy. At Caddo relative tranquillity reigns—at least for the present; possibly it is a tranquillity born of indifference leavened with some sweet reasonableness. Very little is asked of the young people by the school. For their part they reciprocate by asking for very little in return. Instead, they live together at peace with their mentors and at home with adolescent enthusiasm.

Such an accommodation has its price, though, for these same Caddo young people often seemed, during the interviews, unusually ignorant and naïve. That leaves us, then, with a question—whether it is more important to enjoy one's adolescence or to surrender it to the anticipation of one's future—and a hypothesis—namely, were Caddo to be put under pressures such as those at Milgrim would not its potential pot of anger also boil?

Chapter V

TWO SCHOOLS
FOR CONTRAST

DELPHI HIGH SCHOOL

In order to have things right I think everybody ought to co-operate.

A Delphi Student

STUDENTS AT DELPHI are richly endowed. The county in which Delphi is located is reputed to be one of the wealthiest in the whole nation. Its median income for families, at better than $10,000, is by far the highest for the public schools in the sample. Fifty-four percent of the adults in the district have one or more years of college. Over half of those employed serve in high status professional, technical, and managerial positions. Very few of Delphi's mothers work. Those who do, teach or have some other professional position. Altogether, Delphites live comfortably, even richly, enjoying the benefits of an affluent society. They are used to the "good things in life." They score high on intelligence tests. They have traveled, and the majority, including some of the few students registered in the vocational studies program, expect to go to college. A typical Delphi reaction to the Best Thing was,

> The recognition of the importance of studies as opposed to popularity and having a good time. This occurred at the end of my sophomore year. I now realize that more enjoyment can

be found by academic facilities rather than "having a good time."

An untypical reaction was,

I feel adjusted to this school and feel more like trying my very best to give my all in working for my school, both at my studies and outside. The undefinable something called spirit prevails in this school and I *sincerely* hope that other schools may learn the meaning of that word spirit, as Delphi has and thus make themselves better places for young Americans to grow up in.

This response is untypical not through the willingness of a young Delphian to discharge his duty, for this is quite common at Delphi, but rather through the stress on school spirit. For Asher Burke is the only Delphian to mention school spirit. (The emphasis on the word "sincerely" is his.)

The word "routine" appears several times in the responses, as in the following,

The best thing was when I met the Canadian girl I'm going with now. Most everything else around here is routine. This was probably the best thing.

And while not mentioned, "routine" is certainly implied in this statement,

First of all, not very many good things have happened to me in high school. But I guess the best thing that ever happened to me was taking Biology as a Freshman. The teacher was very sharp and funny—the only thing was I didn't learn anything. The whole year was a real blast. All my friends were in my class and we had a ball. We took a field trip to the beach but it was really a beach party. We disected frogs and peeled their skin off and put pieces of the frogs into our enemies' lunch sandwiches. And they ate them. It was very funny but horrible. That was the last time we ever got to disect, for obvious reasons. So this was the best thing that happened to me in high school. I have taken many rough intellectual courses and when the going gets too rough I just think back to those happy days and this helps me to relax.

These are vain, deluding joys—this brood of folly obscuring the melancholy of day-to-day existence. Undoubtedly, and appropriately, there is something thoroughly Apollonian going on at Delphi, some dream that works itself out as routine, enmeshing youth. Oh, for the Dionysiac moment that punctuates the sentence!

Following one of the interviews in Phase II Malcolm Menofee asked permission to stay around a moment. He had a question to ask. "It's about the social situation in high schools," he said, "especially the dating situation." Malcolm then continued,

I've noticed there are several different classifications to daters. One is the fraternity boys who more or less have a girl every week. And another, which I want to know if this is the same in other high schools around the country, is when you start going with a girl, the rest of the students accept this, they accept the fact that you're going with her, there is rarely any chance to change. You are—it may not be actually going steady—it is what I have termed going steadily, in that you do not feel like—you see no way to break from it and change. You may not want to, but even if you did you see no way to change. No one else will date the girl because they have accepted that you are going with her and are not going to start dating her. Does this occur elsewhere or is it generally the same?

After the interviewer answered that he did not know—no one else had raised the question—Malcolm went on,

. . . I am going with a girl, I have been since a year ago, and . . . what I am disagreeing with, or possibly rebelling against is that . . . if I wanted to change, it would be very hard. And there would be—I don't know what the other students would think . . . but they just expect it of you after you've gone with a girl for a couple of days. And while I'm quite happy in my personal situation, I don't believe that this is right, this is, it ties people down too much, and if they should want to change, being afraid of public opinion . . . is enough to— except for the fraternity boys which I think that's even . . . more sickening where you see one boy one day walking down the halls holding hands with one girl and the next day with another, and that just . . . is revolting to me. But this is the thing I want to know about, if you see any . . . possible solution. . . .

After more discussion, the interviewer described the situation as a "sort of conferred . . . informal marriage." Malcolm accepted this,

That's right, that's exactly what I mean. I, I noticed it last year. When you walk up they always leave two seats, when you're—when you walk up to a girl and she's talking to her friends, they walk away. . . .

Then,

. . . you're held together, partly, one thing I've seen—now if I decided, well, I'm not going to go with this girl any more or maybe not to this dance or something, and I go with another girl, first of all, people will be quite surprised. . . . They'll really—they'll start wondering. Second of all, nobody else will take the girl I had been going with. . . .

When asked if he had any ideas on how this institution had arisen, Malcolm answered,

It seems to me that it's just . . . probably springs from the situation in the schools themselves . . . the teenagers outlook on life, . . . "Well, he's . . . striving for something that, striving to settle down, possibly for success . . . and possibly if he is going with this girl, he is identifying this with success and with settling down, so to speak." And I'm afraid this situation does lead to—this is a situation that does lead to early marriages.

Highly specialized as it is, this discussion points again to a weariness that has been institutionalized at Delphi. Here, it is the students themselves who cooperate in pressing toward misery. Consider, also, Brenda Cole's discovery of existential despair,

The worse thing is despair. If I have trouble with my lessons, can't understand, and no time, this is the worse thing.

From whence comes this melancholy that has settled in on these young people so favored in their material circumstances? One possible source is the unsettled lives they have lived. Many of them report that they have moved again and again. This transience associated with a mobile-executive way of life seems to have left its mark. Delphi was the Best Thing to one respondent because,

> This is the first place where we have stayed long enough for me to make good friends (of both sexes).

Other respondents described genuinely happy events in schools they had attended before Delphi. Thus, transience seems to have left its mark. There are, however, other possible reasons to consider for the melancholic mood.

From one perspective, Delphi appears much less oppressive than the five schools already discussed. Delphians are allowed far greater freedom of movement than is customary. Students can use the pay telephones located in the halls during class changes. Corridor passes do not have to be signed—often they are not used at all. There is no real fuss regarding smoking in the toilets. And lunch is for eating, talking, and digesting, not, as turned out to be only too commonplace, simply another opportunity for policing.

With an overall score of 58.0, Delphi ranks relatively low on the ressentiment indexes—just above Ipswich and Havencrest, in fact. A tendency to answer true on items keyed false-as-ressentiment helps account for this low score. Among such items, on which Delphi scores lowest of the low, and significantly, are,

> A club here can invite any speaker it wants to hear, to give a talk at school.
> The school paper is pretty free . . . ; any problems it leads to get thrashed out informally without too many hard feelings.
> The main thing that determines who is in what cliques . . . is whether the members like one another.

Delphi is also low but not lowest of all on,

> The faculty . . . make you feel like they take an interest in students and are there to help if you need them, but they generally leave you alone until asked.

The teachers concur, agreeing with their students that these statements all characterize the school.[1]

A different picture of Delphi emerges when we consider four items on which the students score the school high in ressentiment. These are,

> Some teachers here make you feel like you don't know anything.
> The administration tries to see to it that cliques don't get a chance to dominate in any activity.
> When you miss school for any reason, you have to have a note from your parents to get back in.
> A girl who went too far . . . and got into trouble would be suspended or expelled.[2]

When these four items are examined in conjunction with those presented in the previous paragraph, we find a press that seems free enough on the surface, and yet has a trace of iron somewhere in it. Delphians accept the existence of cliques, and the fact that membership in these cliques implies friendship with other members. But they are also very much aware that such cliques are not to become instruments of power in the school. All six teachers agree with the students that the cliques of Delphi have an enemy in the administration. This is consistent with an impression developed from Phase II testing; namely, at Delphi freedom is allowed the young people in terms of what they can do, but not in terms of how they ought to feel. As the young lady says in the introductory sentence, "everybody ought to cooperate."

"Ought to cooperate" is a key. Delphi is reasonable, by comparison with other schools. There is little pressure about smoking and even less about deportment in the cafeteria. But it is also clear, and made clear, that there are limits. There are rules that carry authority. These are not the administration's rules, however, but rules mandated by the County School Board, to be enforced by the school. To facilitate this enforcement Delphi issues a parents' handbook. In this manual the school (School Board, actually) defines both its authority and the student's duty in such a manner as

[1] Items (20), (34), (14), and (8).
[2] Items (69), (44), (54), and (36).

to make the parent an agent of the Board. Of smoking, the handbook says,

> No student is permitted to smoke in the school building, on the school grounds, or in any area adjacent to the school, or on school buses, while the student is under the jurisdiction of school authorities. For a first offense, a warning will be issued; for a second offense, the student will be suspended from school for a period of five (5) days; for a third offense, the student will be dismissed from school with reinstatement only by action of the County School Board. All smoking offenses are cumulative from year to year. . . .

This, then, is where the iron is, in the rules and regulations imposed by the civil authorities. At Delphi correct conduct demands that,

> Students must conduct themselves in class in such a manner that they will not cause disturbance or annoyance to the instructor or to any of the other students. They are required to be respectful, cooperative, and obedient to the directions of the teacher at all times. Conduct of students when not in class must be normal and above reproach. This includes proper behavior at all social, athletic, or extracurricular activities conducted at the school or under the auspices of the school. Students guilty of overt acts of improper conduct, such as insubordination, disrespect, disobedience, and defiance of authority will be summarily sent home until parental conference may be arranged.

A "boot camp" is what the County School Board intends Delphi to be, a training ground for the executive class. These people sound as if they were used to being obeyed or, at least, used to the illusion of being obeyed. They are not concerned, however, with creating the kind of environment of feeling in which education in the richness of its meaning can take place.

All this contributes to a most complex institutional press. Operating in a situation defined by alien authority, the County School Board, the Delphi administration has succeeded in developing a method for educating that works. Concerned both about its students' needs and about keeping the School Board off its back, the administration has established the school in isolation, shut off from the endangering township and its rigid School Board. The method is inherently unstable, however, in that adolescents, through their youthfulness and their "diversity" (in Erikson's terms), are difficult to contain. To maintain compartmentalization, the students are encouraged to develop self-control. The specific technique may be called "tension reduction through management." Through such management, and in the name of order and the safety of their charges, those in control discourage affect. In this way everything stays peaceful.

As a matter of practice Delphi seeks to avoid crises, to manage tense moments so that no difficulties will arise. To succeed at this the school, in addition to allowing considerable latitude within its walls, keeps a sharp eye out for potential trouble, and, when the management is skillfully executed, intervenes at the right moment against its development. This is done to make certain that problems are handled within the school and that nothing gets out of hand and becomes "a federal case." Such intercession may be through mediation, distraction, or manipulation. It is justified as "for the good of the young people," and in a way it probably is.

There is peace on campus at Delphi, a peace somewhat like that at Caddo, but with a different intent. At Caddo the peace is not maintained out of awareness, but more certainly out of diffidence. At Delphi, this peace is the product of an ominous foreboding. Threatened, the school seeks to produce an Apollonian calm and commits its young people to the maintenance of this calm. Trouble spots are identified as early as possible and those in authority operate to control and reduce tensions emanating from these spots. They manipulate the system so that the ripples of enthusiasm and anger that necessarily accompany adolescence are not allowed to develop into full-blown storms.

While ostensibly practical and in the service of a humane purpose, such tension management carries with it certain dangers. For one thing, it facilitates ressentiment. As opportunities to apply the management technique increase, skill in the use of manipulative authority also increases. To maintain these skills a certain amount of tension-requiring management becomes a desideratum, and for this, ressentiment can be of service. Its calculated devaluing can encourage both mild tension and skill in the managing of this tension. Potentially, tension management can be extraordinarily useful to the ressentient in their malicious machinations, for it is in keeping with their approach, if not with their spirit.

The students also have a lesson to learn if they are to cooperate in preserving the calm. To cooperate, to try for the school, means to adjust enthusiasm to reality, to accept a melancholy duty. Many fine young people, like Malcolm Menofee, have done just this. They have become much like the students we encountered earlier at Hartsburgh and Parma—apt at explaining why whatever is, is right. As a result, even though there may be little actual ressentiment present at Delphi, the tension-management technique has left its mark,

> The best thing that has happened to me is the intellectual stimulation I have received from friends and teachers. I have been made to realize that there are many ideas and opinions besides my own. Some of these ideas have added to and changed my opinions, others I have completely disregarded. I am grateful for each idea I have come in contact with, whether I have accepted it or not, because each idea has helped develop me as a person.

Is it good to be so wise when one is still so young?

HAVENCREST HIGH

> *We experiment here. . . . We will try almost anything if we think it will help get our students involved in their own education. With us experimenting isn't something you do once in a while; it is a way of life, a way we encourage our students to work at thinking, talking, and reading.*
> A Havencrest Administrator

Located in the South, Havencrest has both a warm geographical climate and a sunny institutional disposition. Much of it is outdoors. The classrooms, a spider web of barracks-type buildings, are surrounded by the walks and paths of the campus. Scattered about

are coves and nooks for sitting and talking. The occasional coke machine and the rich growth of grass and shrubs further contribute toward making the school a comfortable place in which to be.

"Comfortable" also describes the homelife of Havencrest students. Reported family income is about average for the sample—which does not include Havencrest's Negroes for they are not yet permitted in the school; the district is not yet integrated. Havencrest parents work in the city itself, at business, at skilled crafts, in the many motels and resorts, and at a nearby federal installation and its associated industries. Many report employments classified as professional, technical, or managerial, and more than a quarter have incomes in excess of $9,000 a year.

One of a group of small, thriving cities somewhat bunched together, Havencrest is close to a major fruit-farming area and is surrounded by resorts. There is no central city associated with it, and it is as cosmopolitan as any of its neighbors. At its liveliest, however, this is a relatively modest form of cosmopolitanism. The annual football homecoming game is possibly Havencrest City's major cultural event.

In their responses Havencrest students are supremely adolescent. They are spontaneous and are not afraid to talk excitedly about love and life. To Bonnie May, the Best Thing was,

When I thought I was in love . . . very happy . . . Whenever I feel as if I'm really learning something or an entirely new thought is presented to me.

The contrast between this statement and the last statement from Delphi is striking, to say the least. Consider Bonnie May's Worst Thing, so forthright, so thoughtful,

I can't think of any bad things that are important or that made any great impression on me. I guess that when a boy I knew was killed in a car accident I really did some serious thinking but really didn't feel too badly about it for death is natural and it doesn't make any difference when you don't know its coming.

When they are not in class, Havencrest students are free to move in and around the school as they see fit; there are no corridor passes. A result of this rare policy of freedom is reflected in the breathless words of Brenda Lee,

> I think the best thing was when I started hanging around with Susie. Cause then I got to know Johnny. In the morning I'll go all the way over to the 1st wing just to see Johnny. Susie's got her 1st period over next to his room. Then I'll run all the way back to the 3rd wing in order to get in before the bell. It gives you a good feeling to know that you belong to a crowd. Mine is the biggest and I talk to everybody instead of being choosey. I think its really sharp the way Haven Hi lets the girls come to school with boys in cars and leave that way. They don't think kids smoking is indecent eitha!

Unlike Delphi, the responses of Havencrest students are infused with positive school spirit and with a real feeling that it is they who count. Charles, who includes on his questionnaire the fact that his nickname is Ronnie, declared,

> The best thing was coming here for school is a whole series of "best things."

To Helene, this was best,

> . . . I learned to speak up in class. I would always be afraid to ask a question or answer any. The teachers make it so easy for you to talk to them.

To most students Havencrest is "Haven Hi." They are proud to be a part of it,

> The most eventful thing that happened to me in Haven Hi was participating in the Concerts given by the music section. It was a wonderful feeling to sing in a group with the auditorium filled with people. When the Concert Choir finished and everybody stood up and applauded I was very proud of Haven Hi.

Another student, almost transferred to another high school, testified to the loyalty students have for Havencrest,

> The best thing that ever happened in high school was being allowed to graduate from Haven Hi. The county built a new high school in my neighborhood and all students living there

were to attend that high school . . . For two years already I have been attending HHS and a new school would not have been "home" to me. But that is not the only reason for most of my friends now attend the other school. The main reason was because of the courses HHS offers, specifically US & World Affairs as well as German II. Besides these classes, the faculty at Haven Hi is, to me, the ideal faculty—enthusiastic, knowledgable, and, knowable as well as having a real interest in me and the world.

Havencrest ranks lowest of all schools studied with respect to the number of Worst Things reported by its students; the average score is 0.97 Worst items per student, in contrast to St. Elmo's 1.53 items and Parma's 1.48. It is also the only school where "Nothing" is the most common Worst Thing response of all, with 17 percent of the students so responding. Second place among Worst Things is personal embarrassment (13 percent), an item category that falls outside the range of the school's authority. After this, Havencrest reactions spread out—almost as if respondents there were searching for things to list—and seven categories are tied for third place. Students at Haven Hi seem to find it difficult to think badly about their high school.

From all the evidence Havencrest is a friendly place to go to school; a joyful spirit abounds and even the negative responses, what there are of them, fail to detract. The results from the ressentiment indexes support this observation, with Havencrest ranking near the bottom for all schools, just above Ipswich. Unlike Ipswich, however, and despite an especially low overall score, there are very few items on which Havencrest differs significantly from the grand average. Instead, the school simply generates relatively low scores on almost every item. Havencrest teachers also agree with their students, and rank their school lowest in ressentiment for all schools.

Among the few statistically significant items for Havencrest is (8). Students at Havencrest affirm that "The faculty here make you feel like they take an interest in students and are there to help if you need them, but they generally leave you alone until asked." On the other hand they disagree with (54), "When you miss school for any reason, you have to have a note from your parents to get back in." In this they differ sharply with Delphi, where such a note is mandatory. Havencrest does not seem to be as concerned with bringing home to their students the extent to which they are dependent on parents as are other responding schools.

Comfortable, friendly, supremely adolescent—these are the words used so far to describe Havencrest. It begins to sound like education there may be largely a matter of making the environment a "lot of fun." This is not accurate, however, for there is considerable interest in things academic. For example, Havencrest students disagree emphatically with the item, "About all that means anything to kids in this school is having a good time." [3] In this response Havencrest agrees with St. Elmo and Ipswich, schools that are notable in having a strong academic press. A similar item on the Stern R Index supports this judgment, as does a report by the project evaluator that a student at Havencrest was reluctant about participating in the testing, despite the stipend, because he "didn't want to miss physics." It is difficult to imagine any Milgrim student showing the same resistance.

So, it isn't all fun at Havencrest. There is a problem, though—one that we have met before. Responses to Phase II testing suggest that young people who are allowed their adolescent ways have difficulty in developing academic facility. Havencrest respondents, like those from Caddo, make many technical errors, are frightfully innocent at times, lose their way in explaining choices on the Q-sorts, and often subside into incoherence. Still and all, the students of both schools are easy to like, and at Havencrest there are notable exceptions to this deficiency. While many students there meander badly, others are positively extraordinary in their brightness and good sense. [4]

In terms of ressentiment, then, are there any negatives at Havencrest? The answer is, yes, there are. Havencrest respondents, for example, agree that "Initiations here are carefully controlled to see that there isn't any rough stuff" and that "The administration has succeeded in getting 'hell week' replaced by 'help week'; pledges go

[3] Item (30).
[4] Tom Tanner and Ken Slocum, for instance, who are quoted at length in Edgar Z. Friedenberg, *Coming of Age in America* (New York: Random House, 1965), pp. 141-147.

out and help in hospitals and such places instead of being hazed."
Also, they disagree with the statement, "The main thing that determines who is in what cliques in this school is whether the members
like one another." Interestingly enough, these items are all focused
on relationships among peers, suggesting that not only is the peer
group important at Havencrest, but that student activities within
their peer groups are a matter of concern for the Havencrest administration.[5]

During Phase II testing, Havencrest students again and again
stressed the values of teamwork and helping. As they saw it they
share in a cooperative venture—the school—working for the good
of each and all. The Havencrest administration approaches the students in this same spirit of cooperation. This is very apparent in
their handling of "dropouts," for example. The students are asked
to identify those among their friends who might be planning to
leave school. Such potential dropouts are then invited to meet with
the Student Dropout Committee, which includes students who have
dropped out and then returned. Together, they discuss the personal
situation of each potential dropout. If it is a matter of more con-
venient scheduling, so that a part-time job becomes possible, the
Committee is empowered to intercede for the dropout and get his
schedule adjusted. If they find that he is under the illusion that
there is money to be made outside, they tell him of their own experiences. They always try to be supportive and to make him aware
of the real consequences of his action. The style is philanthropic in
this social-working society.

There is another significant element in the institutional press at
Havencrest that needs to be singled out—the principal. For Havencrest is a despotism—a benevolent despotism, it is true—but, nevertheless, a place where control is identified with a specific person
and not with institutionalized prescriptions. At Havencrest this
despot has established his school as a separate social compartment,
like Delphi was, but with an essential difference. Havencrest's principal makes a serious effort to involve his students in the life of the
school; he does so to such an extent that, as is suggested in the
introductory paragraph, this effort has become a *modus operandi*.
Consequently his work is never-ending; he must be constantly in-

[5] Items (50), (64), and (14).

ventive, resolute in his dealings with outsiders—the city, the parents, the county and state educational authorities—and enthusiastic in his leadership. For, without constant recharging, such experimentalism could easily lead to cynicism or indifference. Furthermore, his efforts, when successful—and they often are—increase the affectual involvement of the students in their school life. This makes them more difficult to control and encourages some recourse to tension management in the philanthropic mode. Initiations are controlled at Havencrest to make certain that there is no "rough stuff." Having encouraged his students to grow on their own terms, Havencrest's principal has assumed a great responsibility, one that places many demands on his own vitality. And, given his method, he cannot withdraw; he must work at his job all the time. Every place cannot be Havencrest; it is too demanding on its leadership. It is easier, in an administrative world, to operate the way Delphi does, for even though the spirit is dampened the system continues to prosper.

Of all schools, Havencrest is the one most clearly led. In sociological terms, it is a movement, still forming, still becoming. What it can become is still an open question. As at Delphi, the actual procedures used are often ressentient in form, examples being "help week," the stress on teamwork, even the estimable dropout program. These all can be used vengefully, in the best, most pious tradition of ressentiment. It is to the credit of the principal and his aides that advantage is not taken of this opportunity. In this sense, Havencrest is well led.

On balance, the differences between Havencrest and the other schools in the sample are not exceptional; nevertheless, Havencrest is something special. Thanks to the energy and imagination of its benevolent despot it is a good place to grow up in, possibly as good a place as institutional life permits. The young people at Havencrest are allowed to live their adolescence through, and there is leadership strong enough to do the allowing. "My best thing," said Marcia King, "was getting the privilege of going to Havencrest High. I'm grateful for being a student at Haven Hi." The evidence gives little cause to disagree with her.

Chapter VI

THE INDEPENDENT
SCHOOLS

IPSWICH

*No particular incident can be written as one which strongly
bore significance. This school has given me a chance to
look at myself in retrospect. To perfect or attempt to perfect my life as I see fit. My endeavors to this end are influenced quite a bit by my environment here.*

An Ipswich Student

AN INDEPENDENT, coeducational boarding school with students
from twenty states and four foreign countries, Ipswich is unlike any
of the seven schools so far discussed. With a student body of 155 it
is, by comparison, much smaller than the public schools, which
average over 1,000 in size. Two thirds of the Ipswich students live
on the ninety-acre campus, and the other third are day students
from a nearby city. The eleven Ipswich teachers also live on the
campus, either in faculty houses or in dormitory apartments.

Ipswich was founded in 1796 by the Protestant sect with which
it is still associated. It was intended to be a community of learning
devoted to the preparation of young people for college and for life.
In its catalogue Ipswich describes itself,

The school is small enough so that teachers can keep in close touch with each student's progress, but large enough so that boys and girls learn to "stand on their own feet."

Further, the Ipswich catalogue states that,

The development of the finest in each boy and girl is the goal, but it is recognized that this comes only through a degree of self-discipline and in serving in some way the community where one lives.

Personal integrity and friendliness are valued highly. Consonant with this estimable statement of purpose was the Best Thing of one young Ipswichite,

The best thing was that my parents took me out of the terrible conditions that prevailed in public school. Here at Ipswich, I can be myself without being criticized. It has given me the opportunity to become open minded and to understand all types of people and be able to live with them. I have begun to develop my basic principles and along with the prementioned statements, I feel capable of "standing on my own two feet."

Ipswich ranks lowest for all schools on the ressentiment indexes. Scoring 56.2 out of a possible 135, the school places one-half point below Havencrest and more than thirteen points below the highest scoring school of all, Martingale. At 44.2, Ipswich teachers also rate their school very low in perceived ressentiment, only a point above the Havencrest teachers. Unlike Havencrest, however, Ipswich generates a large number of items on which the school score differs significantly from the average for all schools. Altogether, there are 31 of these items on the F-N R Index. On thirteen of these, Ipswich reports the lowest R score of all for the nine schools.[1]

Among these thirteen are several pertinent ones. The respondents agree, for example, that teaching at Ipswich is both serious and competent. At Ipswich, "The teachers who have a good line,

[1] Items (2), (3), (15), (18), (21), (23), (33), (41), (50), (60), (63), (70), and (73). Only items (15), (23), and (21) are discussed here.

who know the latest jokes and who always manage to make the class hour a lot of fun . . ." are not especially liked. Ipswichites are less vigorous than students from other schools in affirming that "Good teachers are the ones who are good to students. They're understanding people who know that teen-agers have lots of troubles and they try to help them all they can." Also, at Ipswich, students are measurably less "discouraged from using their own opinions when answering essay questions." Such responses suggest that Ipswichites are concerned about learning, and think of classrooms as places for serious work. This is confirmed by the project evaluator who reported that classes at Ipswich are consistently conducted on a most superior level. This finding contrasts sharply with his more general observation that there is little that distinguishes one classroom from another in most of the schools.

Ipswich runs to extremes. Among the thirty-one items on which it differs significantly from the average for all schools, there are also eight on which this school has the highest R score of all. As with its lowest R scores these highest are instructive, for they suggest other dimensions to the press there.[2] In agreeing with the glum statement, "Students here often feel like they are butting their heads against a stone wall," Ipswich aligns itself with Milgrim, and against Caddo and Havencrest. Other items affirming ressentiment include the classic statement of ressentiment practice—popular everywhere, but even more popular at Ipswich—which states, "A basic principle of the way this school is supposed to be run is that everybody gets equal treatment no matter who he is." Finally, and odd for a school devoted to college preparation, Ipswich students disagree vigorously that "Our guidance people are really helpful when it comes to advice about careers and college."

Most interesting is the Ipswich response to the student newspaper items.[3] Only 35 percent of Ipswich students agree that "The school paper is pretty free here; any problems it leads to get thrashed out informally without too many hard feelings." At other schools a majority of the responding students felt this to be true.

[2] Items (6), (25), (34), (36), (56), (58), (65), and (68). Only items (25), (56), and (65) are introduced in this discussion.

[3] Items (34), (2), and (18). On (34) Ipswich ranks highest of all schools, and on (2) and (18) it ranks lowest.

Yet, on the other two school-paper items, "The student paper . . . is pretty careful not to print anything too critical of the faculty or administration" nor "to report things in such a way that they might make trouble for the school with other people," Ipswich is much milder in its affirmation than are the other schools.

What does this mean, this contrary response? We interpret it to mean that Ipswich students, while less inclined than most to attribute to the faculty control over their newspaper, are also less inclined to condone such control, should it exist. Taken together, these three items imply a certain tension; and when we add to them the statement that students feel they are butting a stone wall, we become aware of a special sensitivity to authority at Ipswich. Concomitant with this is an image of life at Ipswich contrary to that suggested by the low R score, the fine old tradition, and the frequency with which "coming to this school" was rated Best Thing.

Ipswich responses to the Best Thing-Worst Thing Test are also often ambiguous and sometimes seem especially instructive in their very ambiguity. Consider, for instance, this careful effort at clothing emptiness in rich apparel,

> The vicissitudes of the past years have been such that no event in itself has been outstandingly inspiring or extra-ordinarily valuable. It would be better to say that I found most satisfying the small but personal circle of friends inside and outside of school, who have integrated interests and are both intelligent and intellectual without being counter-conformists or non-conformists.

Why so clever about saying nothing? Another student wrote,

> I have acquired a kind of dignity on entering Ipswich, for I find myself alone quite often and have come to enjoy it. Other students have respected my need and therefore have added much to my personality. I have learned to come out of myself and be cheerful under uncheerful circumstances. I have met someone I like very much.

What can we infer from this about the school as a way of living? A more cunning response was, "The best thing has been the vacations when time is not scheduled."

Ipswich is a boarding school. This fact intrudes and provides one explanation for the gloom since boarding implies both separation and total institutionalization,

> The worst thing was when I had to leave my family in order to get a good education. I don't regret my decision, but it was a painful one, since my family means a great deal to me. Having to leave them, each time after coming home for a vacation, is a terrible wrench. It is less hard now, since I am getting attached to Ipswich, and more secure here. But I'll never forget that first time. I was fourteen and too young. My family drove away crying, as I was, and I was left in the parking lot, to face a whole new world. But I know now that it is a better one. It is a world of ideas, a world of intellectual achievements, and new hope for a very sad old world.

Not all students find it so easy to convince themselves. For Jared Mathews the Worst Thing was,

> Being here at school at the time of Kennedy's death, I was very much affected by this and so were many other people. I would have liked to go home and think about it and recover myself. Here we were forced to go to meetings and assemblies and discussions and it all seemed quite put on.

Ipswich is both parent and teacher to the young people who attend there—*in loco parentis,* as it is commonly said. The press at Ipswich must necessarily enclose more of the student's life than is the case in a home-based school. Added to the classroom press and the extracurricular press, which one finds in any school—Parma, Milgrim, or Havencrest—are the dormitories, the Saturdays to kill, and the limited opportunities to be a different kind of person. These are the kinds of things parents usually are concerned with; at Ipswich, however, the school must be the parent. How well does it do it? It is, it must be reported, nervous, anxious, and not too effective in its parental role. In the section on standards contained in the Ipswich handbook is the following,

> In order for a community to exist, it must operate within a social framework. Regulations have been thoughtfully created to provide for the well-being of the individual. The larger

the community, the more crucial it is that each individual re-spect and carry out his prescribed obligations.

Hard work, sportsmanship, common decency, order, and con-sideration for others are basic pillars of the Ipswich com-munity. Graduation for a senior or future schooling for under-classmen depend on his living up to Ipswich standards during the year.

With this in mind, you are asked to familiarize yourself with the following rules and regulations:

Smoking and drinking are not permitted. Tobacco or alcoholic beverages found in rooms or on one's person are considered an indication of use. Smoking and drinking will be grounds for expulsion. Flagrant disobedience, dishonest academic work, and co-ed dating activity at unspecified times and in unspeci-fied places are also grounds for expulsion.

Following the above passage, dormitory regulations, social rules, and so on, are spelled out in detail. Those in authority mean them, too; many cases of expulsion for infractions are reported. One stu-dent gave as her Worst Thing,

A group of students were expelled from school for breaking the drinking rule. It was the best thing to do for them, to help them grow up, but I missed some of these people. I did not condone their actions, and they received punishment due, but I still felt very sad to see them go.

Many Ipswich respondents are outwardly in agreement with the disciplinary practices instituted by the school authorities. This prob-ably goes a long way toward explaining the very low score on the R Index there. The ambiguity, the cunning, the butting against the stone wall, however, all suggest that in actuality they hold an-other, if covert, position about discipline. The most thoughtful statement of this position was found in an extended, informal dis-cussion on Ipswich conducted by the project interviewer with sev-eral students. Tyler began,

. . . this is our rebellion. . . . Smoking, drinking, sex at Ipswich, even sex, is a rebelling against the rules. It's a hor-rible feeling to sit down and think, well, I'm doing this 'cause I'm rebelling against Ipswich, and then, you think, my father is spending money to send me here, my father is giving me love, sending me here? My father, my parents, are giving me a lot, and giving up a lot to send me to this school, and I'm rebelling. Why?

BURT: And they think it's the greatest thing on earth, this place.

TYLER: And they think they're doing me a big favor, and it —they are doing a big favor . . . but it's—it's hell. And then, you can't question it.

BURT: You couldn't tell them that you would rather go to a public school.

TYLER: Well, that's just it. I wouldn't rather go to a public school. The academics are fine, there's nothing wrong with the academics.

BURT: The academics are wonderful, really. . . . And the kids you're with, the attitude of the kids, their intelligence is nice, it's great. It's much better than you'd find in the public school.

TYLER: But the attitude of the people. In a public school it didn't matter if your teacher was an absolute louse, in your estimation. You saw him for forty-five minutes a day, you shook his hand, you said good-bye, and that was it. . . . But these teachers you got to live with, every day, all day.

Later, Tim joined in,

The faculty have radicals . . . against the students, whereby you have the feeling that someone is just out to get you, and you personally. And they all seem to be zeroing, zeroing in on you. You will have a day where you're hit for everything. From the school dress to where you're just off campus drinking or something. Now this goes both ways. . . . And we strike back equally as hard as we're struck. Is this the atmosphere for study?

This is their rebellion. Against what? It would seem that it is against a system that operates on a different wave length. There is a real feeling of being left out, a need to prove that one is alive, and, at the same time, a feeling of respect for the sacrifices that their parents are making, of fellowship with their schoolmates, and of admiration for the learning of their tutors.

At Ipswich the press becomes strident when it tries to replace the parent. Under the guise of establishing necessary rules for group living it introduces prohibitions designed to satisfy the parents' de-sires—or, at least, what the administration assumes the parents' desires to be. To please the absent parents who pay the bills, the school harasses the present students. Some cooperate, accepting the system and accommodating their thinking to the current ideology. Others, however, are not so readily intimidated and rebel. For the rebels the press becomes a challenge; for those who accommodate, a set of principles. Whichever way they react, all the students are, as one of them said at the beginning of this chapter, influenced quite a bit by their Ipswich environment. One result is ambiguity, often a profound ambiguity,

I lost faith in God and Man—I was no longer a boy which although the best thing was also the worst.

ST. ELMO

I believe the school has a lot to offer in all fields for those who want it.

A St. Elmo Student

According to the school catalogue only those young men "who by their native ability and by their previous academic and personal achievement give promise of future leadership" are accepted at St. Elmo's, an independent day school for boys. Obdurate by princi-ple, St. Elmo is proud of its ancient academic tradition and firm with its students. Attendance at this elite, Roman Catholic-spon-sored preparatory school is held to be a privilege. Authority is vested in the institution, an institution founded on clearly under-stood precepts, and the students attending are expected to respect this authority and guide their lives accordingly. On discipline, St. Elmo's catalogue states,

The registration of a student is an indication on his part, and on the part of his parents or guardians, of his readiness to comply with all the regulations of the school. The discipline, while considerate, must be firm, in order that it may aid in the formation of character. Wanton neglect of schoolwork, disobedience, insubordination, or any conduct which in the opinion of the Faculty is detrimental to the reputation of the school or the good of the student body will be considered grounds for dismissal. . . .

At St. Elmo the rules are clear; their intent is known. Their object is to produce gentlemen,

Towards the middle of Junior year I was chosen to represent St. Elmo at the University Symposium along with a classmate. To attend this I was given two days off from school. When I returned I didn't thank my headmaster for the time off and was reprimanded by him for this.

and scholars,

The best thing happened twice. First in January and then in June. I am talking about the Bulletin Board on which the failures to the final exam are posted. I can remember going to the board each day during test week to see if I failed anything. To my great pleasure I passed everything both times. My only wish now is for it to continue until I graduate.

who are sound in body and in mind,

My best thing was playing basketball for the team last year. We didn't have a good record but we tried and played with all our hearts to acquire the prestige of a school fitting for the trophy we should have won.

At St. Elmo's, the school comes first. The parents, as well as the students, are expected to cooperate. Again from the catalogue there is this about home cooperation,

The authorities in charge of St. Elmo are fully aware that all their efforts for the advancement of the students will fail, unless the parents or guardians of the pupils cooperate with the authorities in securing a compliance with the ideals and regulations of the school. They are urgently requested to insist that their sons devote at least three hours a day to assigned study and review at home. The work assigned each day is carefully calculated and will, as a rule, require this amount of time for preparation. Should a student seem to have less work to do at home, inquiry at the school will invariably reveal that he is neglecting the work assigned and his monthly marks will be found to be correspondingly low.

This rigorous academic press, as demanding on the parents as it is on their sons, is especially interesting in that St. Elmo parents are not what they might, at least superficially, be expected to be—academic themselves, professional people, or in high status executive positions. This is true for Ipswich but not for St. Elmo. The fact is St. Elmo parents are a lot like Milgrim and Caddo parents in the work they do; oftentimes they have such jobs as barber, policeman, liquor store owner, or TV repairman.

The press at St. Elmo is generally clean-cut and on the surface. It functions as a compound of school spirit and strict enforcement. Athletics, for one thing, plays a positive role in the development of this spirit. For O'Hara, the Best Thing was,

> The St. Matthias Game [St. Elmo's traditional rival]. Last year was the most exciting game I've ever seen in my life. The whole school showed up and for the first time everybody felt as a whole. Every single person wanting the same thing so earnestly you could feel it.

Strict enforcement, the other side of the coin, is generally the business of the headmaster, and often the Worst Thing at St. Elmo is an official visit to him,

> Probably the worst thing was my first visit with the headmaster of St. Elmo's. My presence there was not a curtesy call because I was practically ordered down to his office. I had to wait until he was ready to see me. Then I got what I had expected to get, practically murder.

And for another student,

> At the 1962 Thanksgiving Day game with St. Matthias I blew a horn when St. Matthias was playing their school song which was pretty disrespectful and the headmaster made me see my ways.

While the most popular Worst Thing category at St. Elmo's is seeing the headmaster, he isn't the only disciplinarian on campus. The teachers, too, can be rough,

> The worst thing was one day when I was doodling a teacher punished me by taking the pen from me and scribbling all over both cheeks with it.

As a result, pupils at St. Elmo learn to accept authority and, literally, to do as they are told. One young man carried this to its ultimate in answering the Best Thing-Worst Thing Test. John Cardona paid careful heed to the instructions "don't think about it too deeply . . . just put down the first thing that comes into your mind." His reply about his Best Thing states,

> I can understand more fully about the females around me, how they think and act. I was able to go to dances to eventually meet all the girls that I so desire. In High School you have more fun in your teen years by associating with others from other places. Boatrides, football, and basketball games and dances, monthly mixers. And meeting of new friends. If I didn't have to think about it too deeply I would write more of the best things that happened to me in high school.

St. Elmo ranks in the middle group of schools in its ressentiment score (61.2), along with Parma, Hartsburgh, and Caddo. Since all the respondents there are male, and since boys generally score higher than girls, it is justifiable to take a comparative score for boys alone in the nine schools. Such an adjustment places St. Elmo somewhat closer to Delphi, without changing its relative position. It is still fourth from the bottom in rank out of nine schools. The St. Elmo teachers, for their part, rate their school higher on the ressentiment scale than do the students; in fact, they rate it third highest for the sampling, directly below Milgrim and Caddo.

St. Elmo, like Ipswich and Martingale, generates many significant items, including a number at the extreme for all schools.[4] Of

[4] On the F-N R Index, St. Elmo exceeded confidence limits on thirty-three items. On twelve of these the lowest score reported for the item was recorded. These were (1), (16), (19), (30), (31), (36), (47), (55), (57), (59), (65), and (69). On ten the highest scores of all were

the latter the most interesting refer to teacher-student relationships. Both students and teachers at St. Elmo agree that "The students . . . like a teacher to be wrapped up in his subject even though he may demand a great deal from them." This response is clearly consistent with the strong academic press at St. Elmo. Less consistency is found, however, on the response to two other items, for on them the students and teachers disagree. Only 20 percent of the students feel that "Many teachers take pride in the tremendous amount of homework they give" whereas four of the six teachers hold this to be true. St. Elmo is also the only school in which less than 50 percent of the student subjects reported, "Some teachers here make you feel like you don't know anything." Five of the six teachers disagreed and recorded this item as true. Finally, though, both students and teachers agree that "If the faculty . . . think a bright kid is showing off they can be pretty clever at putting him in his place." Clever or not, however, they often succeed,

> In class when talking to a teacher I sounded disrespectful and I didn't mean to be. I hurt him and was disappointed in myself. It was by far the worst thing until I apologized and now he treats me real nice still and it is forgotten.

At St. Elmo the student in the wrong is ashamed. In this he differs from his fellows in the other schools. At Milgrim, as we remember, the student was obstinate, but he had his Record to worry about. At Hartsburgh guilty feelings predominated, and the students were concerned about their Reps and the effects a bad Rep would have on their future. These evaluations are focused on the person exclusively, unlike at St. Elmo, where the person is taught to consider the institution and the ways in which he may have failed it. In this he is closest to Delphi and its melancholy, with the difference that St. Elmoites have chosen their fate—or at least their parents have.

It is a common myth that an education combining firmness with a clear definition of authority reproduces itself; that is, that youths

reported, these being (11), (12), (20), (28), (40), (44), (54), (60), (64), and (66). Of these, only Items (47), (31), (69), and (40) are discussed in the text.

so taught grow up strong and clearheaded. If this were true, it would seem that students at a school such as St. Elmo, where a firm line has been established, would be forged in a hot crucible but one which, nevertheless, should define character precisely and toughen it in the process. At St. Elmo, facts are facts and are so taught. A typical class is a lecture or recitation period; there are answers and they can be learned. Everyone knows where he stands. Consequently, a spirited student, say Gordon Hughes of Chapter I, can test the system to determine its limits and thereby assess his own powers in relation to it. At the same time the academic press at such a school would insist on the development of the intellectual skills Gordon would need in order to master his eventual field of study.

It doesn't work out this way at St. Elmo, however. The skills are certainly developed, but the split we noticed in studying our college science students also appears. There, we remember, those who were best able to tolerate boredom stayed in science while those who thought about the meaning of science left. At St. Elmo, most of the young men we encountered were certainly equipped to tolerate boredom, for they were more than willing to settle for their bowl of lentils. They impressed us as moody, but not concerned. In contradistinction to the commonplace St. Elmoite, Francis O'Toole, a rare rebel who sounds something like an Ipswich student, stated in his Best Thing,

> Nothing too good ever really happened to me. But I think I was most fortunate to get the 2nd and 3rd year English teachers I did. They really made the class reasonably enjoyable and meaningful. They are among the very few teachers here more interested in having students learn about literature, current events, almost anything, rather than just memorizing a lot of boring, meaningless garbage.

O'Toole's Worst Thing is also instructive,

> Last year I wrote a political article for our school magazine which had asked for "controversial" articles from students. As it developed, the Headmaster of the school—who reads and censors every word of the magazine before its printed—didn't agree with my opinions and severely and unjustly punished me.

Against this, place the common St. Elmo response—one that only too often indicates the lack of a sense of justice for oneself. We cite Glazebrook,

> The worst thing happened in freshman year at St. Elmo. Then an unexperienced newcomer, me, joined a rifle club at St. Elmo. This was a new organization and I was happy to be a part of it. However in a few weeks I was summoned to the headmaster along with a number of other boys, all members. We, horrified, found out the club had no official recognition and therefore did not exist. It was a long spell of jug, 5 weeks before we redeemed ourselfs and once more were free from the headmaster.

The young men who attend St. Elmo are training for leadership, or so their catalogue insists. In the course of this training they learn both to obey and to accept the hard tasks assigned them. The school has established a clear line of authority in its press, and from the evidence the students there lend themselves to it. When it squeezes them they blame themselves, and generally let it go at that.

Of the presses examined, St. Elmo's is the most consistent and uniform. Since St. Elmo's parents are also expected to cooperate and agree to such cooperation when they register their sons, there is little likelihood of the kind of conflict between home and school that characterizes Milgrim. This consistency, this one-sidedness, helps to make the young St. Elmoite what he is—when he cooperates, and generally he does. What we found at St. Elmo was a rigorous academic orientation combined with acceptance, self-punitiveness, and a massive sense of shame. We did not find the creative rebellion that tradition suggested we should expect.

Chapter VII

THE PRACTICAL
ATTITUDE

PHASE II testing began with *The Clarke-Barto Incident,* in which Johnny Barto, a reputed delinquent, has been caught smoking in a school washroom. This act of Johnny's is in clear violation of the school rules, and Mr. Clarke, the social studies teacher who has apprehended Johnny, is confronted with a decision of what to do. In accordance with the standard protocol for Q-sort testing, the respondent was then offered nine alternatives and asked to put himself into Mr. Clarke's shoes. None of the nine alternatives was entirely appetizing and many respondents commented that they would have liked to do something nicer had the card comments allowed that. But choose they did, and after choosing they discussed their choices.

Consider, for example, the thoroughly unpopular comment on Card (9),[1] "Mr. Clarke acts as if he hadn't noticed Johnny and leaves the washroom as soon as possible." Most subjects who commented on this card—206 out of the 247 responding to Episode I [2]—argued that if Mr. Clarke did this he would get a reputation as

---

[1] The card numbers have no significance. They were used to identify the card during statistical processing and did not appear on the face of the actual card handed to the respondent.

[2] A respondent could place a card in any of five piles: Best, Good, Neutral, Poor, and Worst. One hundred and six subjects placed Card (9) Worst, and eighty-seven placed it Poor. Only two subjects placed

an easy mark and, further, that everybody would then start smoking in washrooms. To our subjects, the enforcement of regulations, not any internal tendency towards stability, is what protects society from anarchy. Law enforcement is a categorical means of dealing with individuals whose behavior threatens society. Our respondents do not think smoking is wrong in itself, nor do they particularly want to see Johnny punished; but he mustn't get away with anything either.

Other cards rejected by the majority included several suggesting that Mr. Clarke take matters into his own hands. In their responses, students explained that Clarke should always go through channels; they felt that there were specific school authorities who were experts in discipline. Furthermore, Johnny might resent the personal attention implied in the teacher's taking matters into his own hands and might then behave worse than ever. At the extreme, several students pointed out that Mr. Clarke in following such a line of action would expose himself to ridicule and, in certain cases, might even get himself fired or sued.

Our subjects favored comments that combined concern with bureaucratic technique. They stressed that they had tried to select cards that offered the most promising program for "straightening Johnny out," even though there is nothing in the narrative portion of the episode that recommends this course of action. To the great majority of the subjects any change in Johnny that makes him less of a troublemaker and more of a better citizen in school is seen to be beneficial to Johnny. Thus, after the "school psychologist" card —in which Mr. Clarke presents the "Johnny Barto problem" to the school psychologist and the latter then calls Johnny in for counseling—the next most popular cards are those that suggest that Johnny's "case" be referred to a proper authority for processing, that is, that he be referred to the principal or to his parents. This latter recommendation was made with little hope of favorable results. Many respondents expressed a resigned awareness that if the parents or the principal had been able to cope with Johnny earlier they would already have "straightened him out." But something

---

the card Best. These two are Mr. Xavier and Mr. Zorello. Their location in relation to their peers is discussed in Chapter VIII.

did have to be done, the subjects averred, and they had to settle for what was possible.

Thus, results from *The Clarke-Barto Incident* suggest that our subjects, on the whole, are well suited for organized collective life. Too modern for unequivocal self-assertion, they seek and encourage understanding. They see situations as problems to be solved and are willing to support anything that might work. This is the essence of the reflex pragmatism which pervades their response to Episode I of Phase II testing.

Phase I had been designed to tell us about the schools themselves, and the nine school profiles presented in the preceding chapters reported the results of this testing. During Phase II testing we sought to assess the impact that these schools had had on the young people attending them. For this purpose we had constructed the six Q-sort tests, by means of which respondents were to be given an opportunity to express their opinions on a number of pertinent matters related to high school life. *Clarke-Barto* was one of these six.[3]

The six episodes were administered in three separate testing sessions, two episodes a day. Following *The Clarke-Barto Incident* on the first day, the subject was presented with *The LeMoyen Basketball Team,* for which he was asked to think about the appropriate role of a basketball coach. The second day's testing began with an episode stressing extracurricular participation in the planning of a school dance. The other episode on that day required the respondent to choose from among a hypothetical set of his fellows the ones he deemed most suitable for a visit with the king of a country not unlike Denmark. On the final day of testing subjects first completed *Miss Post's English Assignment* and then contemplated the vicissitudes of *Alan Slade and His Friends,* with one of those friends being the aforementioned Johnny Barto. Teacher subjects, for their limited part in Phase II testing, answered the episodes scheduled for the second day, *The LeMoyen Dance* and *The King's Visit.*

Episode II, *The LeMoyen Basketball Team,* places the respondent in the role of Coach Regan of the basketball team and then asks

[3] The complete set of episodes plus directions and results can be found in Appendix B.

him to think about personnel for the team. Excellence and equal treatment of individuals are presented as alternatives here. A newcomer to LeMoyen High, Kevin McGuire, is described in the narrative as trying out for basketball. Kevin's ability, attested to by the team captain, Grant Eubanks, is held to be of a very high order, and he will most certainly be able to make the team should Mr. Regan agree. At present, LeMoyen has four players of championship caliber slotted for starting berths. The fifth position has been shared by five others. If Kevin makes the team, however, these five, stalwart and faithful, will lose their chance to play for they are, at best, mediocre players. Kevin's arrival means Regan will have five stars and no place for the faithful five except the bench.

Both the mediocrities and Kevin are of Irish extraction. They differ, however, in that Kevin is relatively wealthy while they are poor. The story also includes false leads—for instance, that Grant Eubanks is Negro—to suggest that the issue may be one of racial or religious discrimination. It is not, however. Instead, as the story has been contrived, subjects cannot simultaneously nurture the excellent and the deprived through their card choices; they must choose and reveal their values by their justification of that choice.

In answering *The LeMoyen Basketball Team,* and also Episode III, *The LeMoyen Dance,* subjects discovered that they would have to be very precise about the value positions underlying their choices if they were not to be thrown into contradiction. There was no simple problem here for them to solve. This made many of the respondents nervous, and they described themselves as confused. This was a fair judgment, for their answers often were.

Taken as a whole our subjects' responses reflected a strong commitment to the rights of excellence to prevail on the playing fields. The most popular card was (3); 181 out of 247 respondents chose it as Best or Good. It reads,

If Mr. Regan is the kind of coach who puts competence above race or religion, he and the LeMoyen team will surely welcome young McGuire with unmixed delight.

And, correspondingly, Card (8) was least popular, with 192 subjects recording disapproval,

It is too risky to take McGuire on the team, especially if he is as good as Eubanks says he is. Coming from a rich home, and as Eubanks' friend, it would be the last straw for the poor Irish boys. You can't really expect them to take a thing like that. A team may like to have stars, but it needs its back bench, too.

In substance our subjects expressed preferences that supported free access to the team. They insisted that matters such as race and religion were irrelevant and that what counted was a player's ability. After all, many pointed out, there were intramural teams for those who liked lots of action and yet were mediocre athletes.

There are some flaws in this measured response, nevertheless. Most of our subjects reiterated their opposition to racial discrimination, but very few perceived that the story was not *about* racial discrimination and that their comments were not really relevant. They were seldom able to formulate, and were sometimes unable to comprehend, the implications that really were central to the story concerning the probability of economic rivalry among members of the *same* ethnic group arising in the situation described. When they did deal with this problem, they usually dismissed it on the grounds —probably just enough—that McGuire would have sense enough to act like a nice guy and not to think he was superior, so that the difficulty would be concealed or controlled by his upper-middle class social skills. The net picture, then, is of sensible, good-humored young people who do not worry about social dynamics because they know what they have to do in order to get along. As for Coach Regan, they think he should put Kevin on the floor because that will make LeMoyen's victories on the basketball court more certain. And, as for the implied social conflict, who is going to step out of line when the important matter of winning is assured?

On the second day of Q-sort testing, the teachers also participated, and in several cases were interviewed together with their students. Testing began that day with *The LeMoyen Dance*. According to the narrative last year's Spring Dance at LeMoyen High had been something of a fiasco. Certain young men seem to have come only to make trouble. Anxious to avoid a repetition this year, the Student Council is considering changing the format of the dance to make it more elegant, expensive, and exclusive. Before deciding, though, the Council surveyed school opinion, and through its poll discovered that (1) a majority of the entire student body opposes the new plan, (2) the new format is favored, however, by students who attended last year's Spring Dance, and (3) enough students are willing to pay the new price to guarantee that no loss will be incurred.

As usual our respondents were asked to place nine cards containing comments about the episode and then to discuss their placements. They had a choice between going along with an informed electorate, those who attended the previous dance, or agreeing with a majority of the entire student body. Again, as in the case of *The LeMoyen Basketball Team,* they became very nervous and were unsure about the issues involved. Only one card aroused anything like a consistent pattern of response from student subjects. This was Card (8); a majority of the respondents disapproved of the sentiments,

> Unfortunately, the Student Council is not the proper body to get to the root of a problem like this. Youngsters have to learn —sometimes the hard way—to bear the responsibility for their own misconduct. The school authorities should suspend the dance for a year, to teach the students that the privilege of holding it depends on their power to discipline their own conduct. This is a far more important question than what kind of a dance they have.

During their interviews our student respondents did not complain of the mincing, sugary punitiveness of the comment but, instead, of the unfairness of locking the ballroom door after the dance has been stolen; the *tone* of the card, though designed to be offensively sanctimonious, excited little comment. Otherwise, in their response to *The LeMoyen Dance* the student subjects were distinctly uninformative. As their favorite comment they chose Card (7),

> Maybe the dance is pretty corny and crowded. But it wouldn't be fair to turn it into a college-type affair that most of the students would not feel at home at, especially those who have not

had the advantages of the youngsters from better homes. Chaperone the dance a little more closely, if necessary, but keep it down to earth and unpretentious, the way it is now.

They were never very firm, however. In whatever they said, for or against the comments they had chosen, they stuck close to conventional reasoning and in most cases simply repeated back the comment on the card under discussion.

What made their responses to *The LeMoyen Dance* episode unpatterned is not ambiguity or inconsistency in response to any particular card, but the absence of any principle or of any prevailing bias of feeling underlying all their card choices. The opportunity afforded by the episode to discuss the distinction between an electorate per se and an informed electorate was never grasped. Instead, this precise distinction seemed inhibiting, even embarrassing. Our respondents wanted a practical alternative, and, with the two majorities in contradiction, they found nothing practical to settle for.

Contrariwise, the teacher subjects did find a practical alternative in *The LeMoyen Dance* and they embraced it enthusiastically. This was Card (6). Two thirds of the fifty-five teachers agreed with its sentiments,

> Everything the school sponsors is a part of its educational program and should be open to all. It is good for the Student Council to have the experience of running the dance, as this helps them to learn to be responsible. But they must not be permitted to turn public education into an exclusive social affair.

The student subjects, on the whole, were neutral about Card (6).

After completing *The LeMoyen Dance,* our subjects turned to Episode IV, *The King's Visit.* Here the narrative speaks of the impending visit of a king to the state in which LeMoyen is situated. The King's interest in spirited young people is also noted. LeMoyen has been asked by the Governor to send some students to visit with the King and the episode revolves around the choice of delegates for the visit. In substance the LeMoyen student body has been given an opportunity to express an advisory opinion about nine nominees. Each of the card texts accompanying the episode describes one of the nominees being considered for inclusion in the delegation. Respondents to the Q-sort testing, following the conventional procedure, were asked to select from among the nominees the ones they deemed best suited for the visit.

Karen Clarke was chosen Best by both students and teachers. She was described in this way,

> Karen Clarke will be giving the valedictory at graduation for this year's class. As she should. Always well-groomed and polite, she is completely in command of herself in any situation. She is the perfect model of what a high school student ought to be. Her work is neat, correct, and, unlike so many other students', in on time. It really has to be because her dad, Mr. Clarke, teaches here and he makes sure Karen doesn't get any special favors. He makes certain that she stands up for herself and does her work. In student activities she is treasurer of the senior class. She is also a teacher's aide for Mr. Pottitione's chemistry laboratory and a member of the Ethics Committee of the Student Government. Where others are concerned, Karen always tries to be helpful. She wants to go to a good college like Vassar or Smith and plans everything she does carefully, with this in mind. At LeMoyen everybody feels that she has a real chance to get into the kind of college she would like to go to.

Karen was intended to be a person who fits in, who settles for what society demands, and who attunes her aspirations to its terms. She is meant to be capable, but inauthentic. Interestingly enough, many respondents saw her in exactly these terms, that is, they described her as average, more average, in fact, than anyone else. It was for this reason, they maintained, that she was especially suited to represent the school for the King's visit. The strictures about a delegate's being spirited and interesting were ignored entirely. Sending Karen was the practical thing to do; she would best represent what the school was like. And they were probably right.

Notable also in response to *The King's Visit* was our subject's hostility to autonomy. Among the most unpopular choices were Johnny Adams, who could do anything he set his mind to, but only when he wanted to, and Scott Cowen, a brilliant young mathematician who argued with his teachers. Both these young men were depicted as mildly indifferent to personal grooming. This was enough, though, to make certain that our respondents would not have them. "They might not know how to act," it was often said. As most respondents see it, self-directed people are untrustworthy, because they are unpredictable; you can't tell what they are going to do next. Young people who devote themselves to their own inner life and personal interests might work out very well, but why take chances?

What emerges, then, from our subjects' responses to *The King's Visit* is strong further evidence of their pragmatism, with new and important elements of hostility to personal autonomy. Intellectual autonomy is worse than other kinds, but most respondents expressed uneasiness when a pattern of life involved a specialized devotion to personal ends and inner life, whether in jazz (as with the nominee group we called the Combo) or concert music (the forte of Nancy Harris, another nominee). These nominees received short shrift, as did Scott, with his skills at math, chess, and language, or Johnny, who is "not an easy guy to be with." These propensities and traits are not seen as signs of spirit; and those who display such patterns were seldom seen as representative of what is "finest and best about the school."

Again, we should point out that the more individualized young people might have fared better if our subjects had been asked to select the cards as portraits of persons they would like to have had as friends or on any other purely personal basis. But this would have obscured the point that we wished to investigate. We wished precisely to find out whether they could respond to fellow students in a school situation with full respect for the vital and human qualities of the young people portrayed; or whether they would treat the students described on the cards as things—instruments to be used.

Most of our respondents did just that. Their practicality won out over any spontaneity the narrative might have evoked in them. They set up the situation as a problem to be solved—"making a good impression on the King"—and left it at that. To our student subjects, their approach was simply a matter of being realistic; and from what we saw of their schools, they *were* being realistic—

Karen and the other young people they favored would almost certainly have been the ones the school would have sent on an actual King's visit, had one taken place. And, on the whole, teachers agreed, except that they were not quite so convinced by Karen Clarke; while they approved of her they also found her to be somewhat synthetic.

The third-day of testing began with *Miss Post's English Assignment* and ended with *Alan Slade and His Friends.* Miss Post is described in the narrative as a nearly perfect example of the best sort of old-fashioned schoolteacher—a figure who recurs as a minor theme in the American dream. Purportedly, the respondents were asked to complete an assignment she had given. They were to present in class several lines of poetry that they felt best expressed love to them. Nine poems or fragments of poems were offered on the cards, and, following the standard protocol for the testing, they were to choose among the nine and comment on their choices.

Most popular among the several poems were these lines from Sir Walter Scott's "The Lay of the Last Minstrel,"

> True love's the gift which God has given
> To man alone beneath the heaven;
> It is not fantasy's hot fire,
> Whose wishes, soon as granted, fly;
> It liveth not in fierce desire,
> With dead desire it doth not lie;
> It is the secret sympathy,
> The silver link, the silken tie,
> Which heart to heart and mind to mind
> In body and in soul can bind.

Also popular was a verse from Coleridge's "The Rime of the Ancient Mariner" and a verse from a popular song paraphrasing Donne's *Devotion* "No man is an island." Most disliked were these lines from Swinburne,

> No thorns go as deep as the roses's
> And love is more cruel than lust,
> Time turns the old days to derision,
> Our loves into corpses or wives;

> And marriage and death and division
> Make barren our lives.

In addition, a verse from Arnold's "Dover Beach" and two lines from a sonnet by Elizabeth Barrett Browning were not liked.

Perhaps the most revealing responses elicited by *Miss Post's English Assignment* were made by most of our subjects before they had even sorted the cards. This episode, alone of the six, produced rather widespread embarrassment. Our subjects frequently said that they disliked poetry and did not understand it; it made them uneasy. They did not respond with embarrassment to the story of *Alan Slade and His Friends,* which refers to elements that seem far more likely than the few verses of the assignment to arouse anxiety. Nor did they actually have any difficulty such as they did with *The LeMoyen Dance,* in handling the task when they actually undertook it; most of our subjects showed consistent, if often atrocious, poetic taste.

Miss Post presents the one situation that our subjects do not treat as a problem. They do not use the information that they are given about Miss Post in order to figure out choices that would please her or "make a good impression." What they prefer is love that is expressed sweetly and innocently, whether this could be expected to appeal to Miss Post or not. They are attracted by the denial of aggressive sexual intent in Scott's line "It is not fantasy's hot fire" and by the assertion that God is the source of love, which reverberates through their reasons for favoring the three most preferred poems. Thus throughout the comments to the assignment Miss Post's request for emotional authenticity is ignored. Instead, eschewing practicality for the moment, our subjects lapsed into sentimentality.

In *Alan Slade and His Friends* the lead narrative is long, complicated, ambiguous, and replete with subtle cues—in effect, as one subject said, it is a complete soap opera in itself. As a continued story in a newspaper, it could be synopsized in this way. "During her senior year at LeMoyen High, sweet, lovable Monica St. Loup asks Mr. Blakely, the dean, to speak to fellow senior, able, attractive Alan Slade about his unfortunate association with the notorious hood, Johnny Barto. The dean then calls Alan in for counseling. Subsequently, Alan drifts into ennui and vaguely loose living. His grades drop and he does not respond to the dean's interest and concern. The school psychiatric consultant, Dr. Bruch, recommends psychotherapy. Alan's parents (his father is an attorney) think differently, however, and make little effort to cooperate. They maintain that there is little wrong with Alan that is not explained by Dean Blakely's unwarranted invasion of their son's privacy. Johnny Barto, for his part, after a talk with Dean Blakely, drops out of school altogether and leaves town." This is where the narrative leaves off. The comments on the cards refer to the relationship between Alan and Mr. Blakely.

In the fullness of their practical mode, our respondents made this story into a problem and dealt with it accordingly. Because this response leads us into more serious matters, demanding a more thorough analysis, we have relegated it to the next chapter. So far, the observations that we have reported relate primarily to our general impression after hours of interviewing, and prior to the time when we sought to treat the data systematically. From this impression, except for *Miss Post's English Assignment,* we have found our student respondents practical in all things. Now, to *Alan Slade and His Friends.*

Chapter VIII

THE LEMOYEN
CONTEXT

By THE TIME a subject had come to *Alan Slade* he had had a great deal of experience with the Q-sort method and should have been over any confusion or fears he might have had regarding the procedure. He knew the interviewer and had some awareness of the direction in which the discussion was moving. For these reasons we thought that the results from *Alan Slade,* reflecting a considered opinion on the part of the respondent, ought to be somewhat more dependable than those from earlier sessions. As a result, we took responses to this episode most seriously.

For *Alan Slade and His Friends* the comment most often placed Good or Best by our subjects (Card [2]) refers to what they perceive a proper relationship between parent and school to be. It states,

> The attitude of Alan's parents illustrates how necessary it is that parents cooperate with the school, if as much as possible is to be done for students when they need help. In a world as interdependent as ours, the individual must cooperate with the legitimate institutions of society if progress is to be made.

Out of 245 respondents, 194 approved and 9 disapproved of this comment, making it one of the three most favored cards of all for the entire six-episode Q-sort distribution. (There were fifty-four cards in all, nine for each of the six episodes.)

Many respondents went so far as to endorse this statement as a moral imperative—Burt Holland of Milgrim for one. Soft-spoken, well-mannered, but shy, Burt is an eleventh-grader in an academic program, with a B– average. His father works for the sanitation department. In many ways Burt is an average young man, and our statistical measures place him very close to the grand average for all students in his overall card choices. Burt commented,

> I think it very necessary for the parents to cooperate with the school because the boy apparently has something the matter with him and the school should be able to get the parent's cooperation in the case. It shouldn't be just a case of finding out about it as—as we hear so much of—that the parents know something's the matter with the boy but then either are too democratic with him or just completely . . . don't do anything about it. I think the statement here, "In a world as independent [sic] as ours, the individual must cooperate with the legitimate institutions"—I think that covers it pretty well, that they should, if the school tells them, they should look into it, even if it doesn't seem to—if they don't think it's true, they should look into it.

Other choices favored by students for the *Alan Slade* episode included (1),

> Bad off as he seems to be, the root of Alan's trouble is probably basically self-pity. Certainly, he is lucky at least to have both a friend and a counselor so devoted to helping him. If he won't let them, he can't expect things to get much better.

and (6),

> Mr. Blakely seems to be on the right track; but the school's resources do not extend far enough to back him up. When the school psychiatrist recommends that a student be given psychiatric help, the school should require that he accept it and, if necessary, provide the funds for facilities to make it possible.

Each of these cards was favored by more than 50 percent of our respondents, and only one fifth or less had doubts about them as appropriate comments.

To most respondents Johnny Barto was pretty much a lost cause and, worse than that, was contaminating. On the whole our subjects were decent young men and women and had they had anything constructive to offer in Johnny's case they would certainly have called it to our attention. Something needed to be done and be done promptly, too, they felt, if Alan was to be saved from being drawn down the primrose path by Johnny. And that was where Mr. Blakely came in, for it is especially the dean's intent to be helpful that legitimizes his intervention. As a result, over one half the students disapproved the indignant comment (Card [7]),

> Mr. Blakely's action is both unprofessional and a gross invasion of privacy. He is allowing himself to be influenced by one student against another, has used his office to break up a private friendship between two students, and done grave injury to both. To call this "helping" is either hypocrisy or lunacy.

This they found unacceptable, despite evidence in the text clearly supporting the card's interpretation of the situation. The point is that Mr. Blakely is just doing his job; and since he is doing his job the Slades are obligated to cooperate with him.

As parents, the Slades came off badly. While they did not excite marked hostility from the respondents, they were usually dismissed as flawed. Particularly striking to us was our subjects' refusal to see them as loving, concerned parents, although we thought we had clued this idea into the narrative. They were seen rather as defensive and punitive—an irate mother and father who are angry at Blakely because his view of their son stigmatizes them as bad parents.

We made *Alan Slade and His Friends* ambiguous partly to improve its projective character, partly to reduce its possible offensiveness, but chiefly to see whether our respondents would be deterred from intervention by the fact that the story did not make it quite clear what they were intervening in. They seldom were deterred. It was those very subjects who most stressed the Slades' obligation to cooperate who often were most bewildered as to just what was supposed to be wrong with Alan. Others distorted the time sequence, which is explicit but deliberately presented out of chronological order. Such subjects would infer that Mr. Blakely had called Alan in *because* his grades were falling—even though the story states that Monica consulted the dean "before anyone else had even noticed Alan's need for help."

The great majority of our respondents to *Alan Slade and His Friends* affirmed an acceptance of conventional authority vested in an institution. They also favored a reduction of conflicts to stereotyped terms. Both Alan and his parents are expected to display a low degree of personal emotional involvement. Should the family act otherwise our commentators considered such deviant action a defect of character. All this followed a trend already apparent in the five earlier Q-sort episodes.

In *The Clarke-Barto Incident* Johnny Barto was thought of as a problem. There, the school psychologist was supposed to tinker with him and straighten him out. For both *The LeMoyen Basketball Team* and *The LeMoyen Dance* our respondents experienced difficulty making practical choices, due to the contradictory nature of the cards. In their answers to Episode II they spoke of wanting *both* a winning team, even though this might encourage exclusiveness, *and* an open society situation where no one would be excluded. And they seemed to feel that good administration ought to be able to achieve both ends. They further complicated their task by introducing an essentially irrelevant issue about racial discrimination, one designed so that its defense demanded cant on the respondents' part. They spoke cant easily enough. Even though the choices did not allow for compromise, they were not deterred. Being practical young men and women they accepted the contradictions of their position with aplomb, and talked on, in comfortable innocence. A somewhat similar solution developed out of *The LeMoyen Dance*. Essentially, they stuck to the conventional throughout their interviews despite an apparently greater confusion and sought means by which the situation could be manipulated so as to allow for adaptation to it with a minimum of sweat. There were of course impressive exceptions to the commonplace responses on these two episodes, just as there were on the other four.

For *The King's Visit* most respondents evinced a marked preference for "all-around" persons over those who focus intensity on their efforts. They were also concerned that the person chosen be a good representative of the school—more concerned, in fact, than they were that he fit the King's specifications of "spirited" and "interesting." Only when we reached *Miss Post's English Assignment* did we find our subjects indifferent to practicality. For that episode, the respondents did not tailor their choices to Miss Post. Instead they lapsed into sentimentality. Sentimentality, of course, is also associated with conventionalism, so we did not think this lapse too significant when we first encountered it.

On the whole, then, we found the majority of our subjects conventional in their responses and conventional in exactly the terms used earlier in the study. This majority also turned out to be a formidable majority, as we discovered when we measured the distance that each respondent stood from the grand average for all respondents.

Since it was possible to place any specific card for an episode in any one of five positions ranging along an axis from Best to Worst, we were able to compute a Grand Average Pile Placement (which we call GAPP) for each card. For example, 4 respondents chose Card (1), Episode I, as Best, 33 as a Good choice, 110 were neutral, 90 found it to be Poor, and 10 thought it Worst. By rating these choices along a 9-point scale with a range from $+ 4$ to $- 4$, we determined that the GAPP for Card (1) was $- .67$. The set of these GAPP's, taken together, constitutes the grand average position for the whole deck.

We then measured the distance each subject stood from this grand average. Again, using Card (1), let us say that a respondent was one of those four who had placed the card Best. On the 9-point scale he stands $+ 4.67$ from the GAPP $(- .67)$. Computed as D^2 (the distance squared, to remove signs) his rating for the card would be 21.8 (4.67×4.67). Had he placed the card in the neutral pile his D^2 distance for this card would be .45 $(- .67 \times - .67)$. Not only does a respondent have only five alternative piles in which he may place a card, but he is also limited with respect to the number of times he may use any one pile. When chosen, the pile placement determines the D^2 value to be added to his overall score. Thus, on completing the six episodes a respondent will have placed fifty-four cards, each of which will have a D^2 distance value. When these values are added together, they give him his overall D^2 score—and thereby measure his distance in units of D^2

from the grand average. The minimum attainable score possible is
90.1, the maximum is 811.4. The D^2 score for Miss Arbuthnot of
Hartsburgh, who was the respondent with rank order (1)—that is,
the respondent closest to the grand average for all subjects—was
121.0, while rank order respondent (245), Mr. Zorello of Milgrim,
who stood furthest from the grand average, scored 449.3.

In Table 2 the D^2 scores and card placements for six strategically placed subjects are compared directly with those of Miss Arbuthnot. The six to be compared include Miss Bates, ranking second—that is, next most average; Miss Ingram, ranking (82), the

Table 2. Q-Sort Test Data: Comparison of Six Strategically
Located Respondents with Rank Order Respondent One (Phase II)

Respondents	Rank Order	Categories of Response			D^2 from Arbuthnot	D^2 from Grand Av.
		Agree	Doubtful	Disagree		
Bates	(2)	37	16	1	173.5	131.2
Ingram	(82)	30	20	4	296.0	205.6
Stein	(163)	26	20	8	415.5	248.6
Xavier	(243)	23	24	7	520.3	412.0
Young	(244)	18	24	12	669.0	427.8
Zorello	(245)	22	21	11	629.3	449.3
Expected*		18	24	12		

Agree: two subjects both favor a card, including Best-Best, Best-
Good, or Good-Good, or they both place it neutral, or, similarly, they
both disapprove of a card; for instance, a Worst by Miss Arbuthnot
and a Poor by Mr. Zorello constitute agreement.

Doubtful: one subject favors or deplores a card while the other places
it neutral.

Disagree: a contradiction in choice; for instance, Miss Arbuthnot
places a card Good and Mr. Zorello places the same card Poor.

* A range of expected placement, were chance the only factor, is included for purposes of comparison. It was calculated from a 9 × 9
matrix including all possibilities.

boundary of one third of the subjects; Mr. Stein, ranking (163), the boundary of two thirds of the subjects; and the three most atypical—Mr. Xavier, Miss Young, and Mr. Zorello.

Clearly, disagreement is never very strong among the respondents. Even Zorello, a brilliant, articulate, terrifying auxiliary subject (see page 22) reaches only a little beyond the central position as defined statistically. Miss Young is the only individual who actually achieves the most likely distribution in relation to Miss Arbuthnot; all the others are closer to the centroid respondent. The two thirds of the subjects closest to the grand average enclose a D^2 range of 126.9 points. Mr. Stein, their boundary subject, differs with Miss Arbuthnot on only eight of fifty-four cards. The top third of the subjects—those with the highest D^2 scores as computed from the grand average—add another 200.7 points in D^2 value. The span between Miss Ingram and Mr. Stein is especially crowded (43.0 points on the D^2 scale), suggesting that the sample as a whole can be characterized statistically as agreement in general and mild disagreement on particulars.

We began this study by proposing that schools that are perceived by their students to have highly ressentient practices and procedures would contribute relatively few subjects to a putative adolescent cluster, since ressentiment, in its very essence, is hostile to adolescent exuberance, craftsmanship, and authenticity. In schools where students find themselves harassed by ressentiment we assumed that the risks involved in embracing adolescence would be very great. Young people in such schools, we felt, would be driven by a chronic anxiety either into conventionality or into eccentricity and privatization—and hence into our "residual category." Conversely, in schools where students feel the press of ressentiment but lightly, adolescent exuberance and self-assertion are unlikely to be blocked by punishment and should be characteristic concomitants of human growth. Conventionality is fostered by so many powerful forces in our society that it, too, should be prominent, though less so than in a highly ressentient social climate.

These expectations were basic to our research design. They have not been fulfilled. When our data were examined both qualitatively and quantitatively we found no discernible adolescent cluster. Indeed, we found no clusters at all, neither adolescent nor residual. Instead, we were swamped with conventionals. Our entire Q-sort sample of 245 subjects includes no group of as many as three individuals distinguished statistically by a pattern of card choices common to themselves and distinct from their peers. The interviews, moreover, showed clearly that this was no artifact; our respondents not only picked the same cards but they gave much the same reasons for picking them. They also selected comments that primarily expressed a conventional position, as illustrated by our discussion of *Alan Slade and His Friends*. Of course, many of those located at the statistical outer limits are thoroughly unconventional and were especially so during their interviews. They are also idiosyncratic, however, and to an extent that confounds classification. They are both adolescent and residual, and in most complex proportions.

The insistent conventionality of the central mass of our respondents raises a question that looms large in any study of attitudes and values, especially when a socially subordinate group such as high school students is studied: that is, to what extent can we be certain that the subjects were expressing their true beliefs and not just telling the interviewer what they thought he wanted to hear? In the case of this study we cannot be sure, but there are reasons for believing the question to be less than crucial. The most obvious rejoinder is simply, "If they wanted to tell the interviewer what he wanted to hear, for God's sake, why didn't they?" No outcome of the study could have distressed us more than the responses most of the subjects actually gave.

There is also a fundamental reason, however, why the possibility of faking seems to us unimportant. If a subject is not really conventional and submissive but only chooses to submit in order to please a strange interviewer with no power and no wish to constrain him, then surely he is indeed conventional. It is simply too late in the century to take much reassurance from the good guys who go along with the system out of canniness and courtesy, even though they personally reject it. Such people may be socially useful as administrators, valuable in reducing friction and centrifugal force in a society that imposes frustrations on everyone and gives few occasions to rejoice. But what do they add up to? Too little, we fear, to justify the rejection of any null hypothesis.

Results from the schools also proved discouraging to our expectations. A credible statement anent ressentiment in the schools would be that evidence of a considerable number of actions which are essentially ressentient were uncovered, but certain processes associated with the institutional presses themselves complicated the results to such an extent that they discourage organization of the data into a consistent pattern. Ressentiment was shown to be present everywhere, even at Havencrest and Ipswich, but it takes subtle forms. It was not readily disentangled from the processes that are.

No adolescent cluster was generated by statistical analysis, and for that reason we have no cluster to compare with the ressentiment rates. We can break down into thirds the results from the Q-sort testing, as was done earlier in this chapter, and, by that means, develop a putative adolescent cluster. By now the reader should be familiar with the particular nature of each school's press and can judge for himself the extent to which the ressentiment rate represents a true measure of the ressentiment in a given school. Table 3 compares these rates with the Q-sort results.

Table 3 records first the mean score for each school for the ressentiment index, and, then, in three columns, the number of subjects each school contributes to each third for the Q-sort testing. Column I contains those closest to the grand average for all students and Column III those furthest from it. Thus, Column I includes those students we deem most likely to be conventional, in that they are closest to a common position, and Column III those we deem most adolescent. While we cannot insist that the highest third are adolescent, the Mr. Zorellos, the Miss Youngs, and the Mr. Xaviers are, at least, statistically different in their responses from the common run. And, basing our judgments on their interviews, we can also assert that in our opinion these highest third respondents are clearly the most exhuberant and self-assertive of all.

Reference to Table 3 shows that St. Elmo and Hartsburgh have produced the highest number of conventionals, despite their average ressentiment scores. Milgrim and Martingale both produced a great number of adolescent respondents, and the highest ressentiment scores. Ipswich also produced a large number while generating one of the lowest ressentiment scores. And the results from the

Table 3. Comparison of Ressentiment Data (Phase I) and Q-Sort Data (Phase II)

School	Mean R Score	N in Each Third			Total	One Third of Total
		I	II	III		
Martingale	69.6	5	9	11	25	8.3
Milgrim	69.2	5	6	13	24	8.0
Parma	63.1	9	15	5	29	9.7
Hartsburgh	63.1	12	8	5	25	8.3
Caddo	63.0	8	8	9	25	8.3
St. Elmo	61.2	14	8	3	25	8.3
Delphi	57.9	9	10	6	25	8.3
Havencrest	56.9	9	6	9	24	8.0
Ipswich	56.2	7	7	11	25	8.3
All Schools	62.4	78	77	72	223	73.3

The exclusion of the auxiliaries accounts for the discrepancy in the total between 245 and 223 as well as for the uneven distribution of the thirds. The auxiliaries were included when the thirds were originally computed.

two schools, which, when profiled, seemed the least exacerbating, Caddo and Havencrest, are equally confusing. From this it is clear that Table 3 offers no comfortable correspondence between the ressentiment scores themselves and the results from the Q-sort testing.

A subtle structure, not a simple one, is what is indicated. Originally, in thinking about the schools, we had in mind an integrated institutional system, developing its press in an orderly manner, with a modest vagueness at the edges. As a result we very much underestimated the extent to which the institutional structure of the school was not simple. We had presumed the existence of an acknowledged Establishment, which would be taking a firm hand in establishing the way the school was run. We did not find one, except at Havencrest and St. Elmo. Instead, what we found was always more complex than what we had expected.

Our awareness of the contrary nature of the schools began with Parma. There, we discovered a confusion of objectives and an odd two-sidedness to everything associated with the Parma Way. At the time we attributed this, provisionally, to a new-old problem unique to Parma and assumed that there was some difficulty at that school in coping with a changing community. Terming the difficulty "ambivalence," we left it at that.

At Hartsburgh, which turned out to be as new and as old as Parma, the Establishment was apparently sounder but, as the incident of the disciplinary assistant principal suggests, probably still in a state of flux. So we went to Milgrim. There, a battle royal was in progress, with the Establishment standards in direct conflict with those that the young people had brought with them from their homes. Lines were being drawn and positions hardening. As a result of our observations at Milgrim we decided that incongruity was the nature of the system. The school Establishment, however constituted, apparently did not have a firm grip on the controls. Thus, we came to accept incongruity as a matter of course. At Caddo the students were pleased whereas the faculty often was not. At Ipswich, with the young people raging against the dormitory life, the fur was flying thick and fast. And at Delphi the school managed its internal tensions with great facility, and mediation had become a *modus operandi*. Only St. Elmo had established a simple line of authority to which all students were expected to adhere.

Every school studied was a compound of forces that had become reified into social entities. Parties contended—the administration, the teachers, the principal, the students, the public authorities, and the parents. Each school, it seemed, was a vortex of disagreement, and it was out of such a complex that the actual school was constituted. The school was more the construct of these forces than it was the product of an educational philosophy. There was no simple structural press per se; there was instead a polymorphous structure of contradictory forces which the Establishment, such as it was, and for better or for worse, attempted to manage with a minimum of "trouble."

Our original error lay in attributing power too exclusively to those elements of the polymorphic structure that possess formal authority. In most schools those with such formal authority—the putative Establishment—most likely would appreciate being able to exercise authority decisively, as they certainly did at St. Elmo; however, our information suggests that it is exceedingly difficult to maintain a cogent position when so many loci of power exist. Instead, at schools other than St. Elmo the constituted Establishments settled for what they could do and let it go at that. At its most friendly we have the Delphi or Havencrest system of isolation; at its most controlling, the Hartsburgh cooperative venture in citizenship.

All the participants to some extent collaborate in complicating the structure. Generally the students are in the weakest position of all. Nevertheless, even out of this weakness some force can be generated. At both Milgrim and Ipswich the students were often tough-minded and intransigent; and at Martingale they were surprisingly shrewd in the way they worked with their predicament. As the research developed it also became clear to us how important parents were and that, as at Parma and Ipswich, it was often their support that had made possible what independence of spirit there was. Judging from this one would expect that the situation *vis-à-vis* independence of spirit would be especially difficult for the young men of St. Elmo, for there the parents as well as the boys were expected to cooperate with the Establishment.

Parents may also play an entirely different role, however—although not always by their own choice. To some degree all the schools studied conceived of themselves as surrogates of the parents and as defenders of the community morality. The teachers imagine what the parents demand and act accordingly. Whether this image, a product of conventional wisdom, reflects the actual position of the parents is rarely examined. Just as rare is any consideration by the teachers of their proper role as educators with a responsibility for the clearsightedness and intelligence of the whole community. Instead, the teachers describe themselves as duty-bound to defend in the name of virtue what ought to be. The parents of the children who favor Card (2) of *Alan Slade* are not likely to think much differently themselves. Indications are that they also believe in experts. As a result, most schools commit a certain amount of psychic violence in the name of an elusive image of propriety. This they do in all good conscience, too. Appropriate or not, such propriety as is demanded becomes in its own way a contributing element in the emerging institutionalization.

The parent role, albeit complex in itself, is only one locus of power; another is that of the teachers, who also support, neglect, or acquiesce in the face of the pressures generated. And, as the example of Havencrest indicates, the principal has his role too. (There, though, he uses it creatively to resist the conventional wisdom of the community.) In sum, then, in each school a set of contending forces, exhibiting different forms with energies at different angles, expresses itself in combination as a unique situation. Each of the public schools is the product of a state law, an instituted public authority, a community of taxpayers, a particular administration, teachers, parents, and students, all individually, collectively, and severally. The independent schools have like origins.

The school itself is realized as a dialectical synthesis, elaborated as the conscious invention not so much of a single master established against a single set of servants as it is of a variety of masters, both real and imagined in their power, and of a variety of servants who are also masters. Intricate, awkward in terms of its object, flawed, perverse, and uncomprehending, the polymorphous structure emerges out of this contention, as the participating master-servants, servant-masters recognize through their acts and their reflecting on these acts, the dimensions of their predicament and, in terms of their vision and their concern, act again.

The simpleminded ressentiment we began with has been replaced by this emerging kaleidoscopic context of structure. Where, in this institutional press, which is far more complex than had been anticipated, would Gordon Hughes have an opportunity to grow into his full vigor? How is ressentiment actually infused into such a press and what are its effects? These we will now consider.

Chapter IX

MISS POST'S
ENGLISH ASSIGNMENT

IN A WORLD as interdependent as this one is, how do those in the bloom of their youth respond to two lines taken from a love sonnet by Elizabeth Barrett Browning?

> When our two souls stand up erect and strong,
> Face to face, silent, drawing nigh and nigher.

Well, several of the young people said that they did not like them especially. Two or three indicated that they didn't know what "nigh" and "nigher" meant. One youth missed the point entirely and saw the opposite of love in these lines,

> There's no affection in it. It's, like, it could be just two men coming together with swords and everything. It doesn't show any emotion or affection towards a person.

More common, though, were remarks like Jean's. She said of this excerpt from the sonnet,

> It's short and it seems to just leave you off, blank. It seems very cold. It doesn't express anything. It just says two sentences. . . . It wouldn't mean anything to me if I were to read it in a book.

Brenda, although also commenting in this vein, was less sure of herself,

. . . it didn't give me any concept of what it was trying to put across. It was supposed to be about love. . . . It doesn't necessarily represent any kind of love, except maybe . . . physical love. . . . That's the only thing I could possibly get out of it.

These same two lines made Sharon nervous,

I didn't like this one because it had some feeling but there was something very tense and very emotional and I don't feel that love is always tense and emotional. There are silent types of love, too, I think.

These are the commonplace responses to this too-short segment from *Sonnets from the Portuguese*—a sample of those who stand close to the core of averageness. Asked to define love through poetry they saw these lines as wrong.

Alan, however, felt differently,

As it says, drawing nigh and nigher. . . . It just sort of gives this feeling of every minute . . . the amount of love increasing and the idea of it growing . . . more. This is really talking about a growing love. It's awfully emotional.

And, for Jo Ann, two lines were sufficient,

Mostly, when you think of love, it's hard to explain. . . . It's something you don't really talk about to people. I think of two people that are in love. If you're with a person that you're very close to . . . you have this mutual bond between you. You can, as it says, stand erect, face to face, without talking to each other and still understand the problems that you have. I liked it because it was short and I think that something as huge, as encompassing as love . . . that you can't write a whole book about it and explain it . . . and that something that's short and just makes you think of one thing is better.

But the Alans and Jo Anns are rare in our sample. Most of our subjects found the Browning excerpt from *Miss Post's English Assignment* too short and too strange and rejected it. Only 13 percent of the respondents favored it as against 48 percent placing it Poor or Worst.

This raises a question. Jean and Brenda and Sharon, these fussy little old maidens who must have everything spelled out, can it be that they are oblivious to the passionate imperatives of their day? Do they not listen, and twist, and succumb as the Supremes command, "Stop in the name of love,/ Before you break my heart"? [1] Are they indifferent to the tortured pathos of their nasal bard, Bob Dylan? Are they deaf to the cruel bondage, to John Lennon's imploring, "If I fell in love with you,/ Would you promise to be true?" [2]

They must. We are certain they must. We have as testimony the wild receptions for such as the Rolling Stones, we can sense the Dionysiac intensity of James Brown, and we can see in the eyes of teenage damsels the purity of their affection for Herman's Hermits. If our commonplace respondents are at all like the young people of their day, they are then quite the opposite of what their comments imply; they know every word of every song, they can capture every cadence of the rhythm in their bodies, they drench themselves in romance. How, then, could they not have understood Elizabeth Barrett Browning?

There is a simple answer, of course. They lied. They didn't tell the truth about themselves; or, and what is more likely, they left a different truth about themselves at home.

The contrast between rock and roll and the responses to Miss Post is too striking to be ignored. The love that Jean and Brenda and Sharon share in their comments is a gentle, placid pool of sentiment. To Brenda this love tastes cool and even refreshes,

> . . . the silver link, the silken tie, that's a kind of love that is represented in my heart as a soft . . . kind of clear, crisp . . . feeling and I don't know, this seems to be . . . the type of love that I guess a man would feel for a woman.

On the other hand, the love of rock and roll is vital, moody, intense, as much a part of its beat as it is of its words. The two loves, the vital and the gentle, cannot be mistaken for each other. They are more than contrast, for loyalty to one endangers the other. [3]

[3] No formal proof of the existence of the vital love and its contrast

Jean and Brenda and Sharon cannot be absolved. They certainly know of the other love, and, even more certainly, they dream of it. Nevertheless, when asked, they denied its relevance to the assignment and lapsed into sentimentality. This, we maintain, was because the tests that they took for the project were administered in school. They had no intention of lying, and were their lie pointed out to them they would probably act flustered and remonstrate. But, they knew that they were in school, and *there* one answers according to the school way of thinking and acting; no hand-holding and all that. They also knew that the spirit and the beat of rock and roll belonged at home, and they left it there. So, they lied. Let us consider the implications of these innocent lies.

Until our respondents encountered *Miss Post,* they had proved themselves practical in all things. When faced with an episode, they first sought to ferret out the problem implied and then set about solving it in the most expedient manner possible. Yet, with Episode V they shifted abruptly into what appeared to us to be a pious sentimentality, unlike themselves. They did not respond in a manner calculated to appeal to the teacher named Elsie Post.

We were surprised by this retreat into sentimentality. We had expected that *Alan Slade and His Friends,* with its muted, faintly dubious overtones, might unsettle our subjects, but never that the episode of pure, decent, conscientious Miss Post would. She did, however, and as a result our subjects chose, it seemed, *not* to treat the episode as a problem to be solved. Instead, they drifted off, into cant. They denied the possibility of Elsie Post, the person, and

---

to the gentle love is offered. Instead, we ask the reader to turn on his radio, turn up the volume, and listen. Listen to the Beatles, for instance, or the Supremes. If you have difficulty understanding them, the texts can readily be recaptured with the help of almost any intelligent young lady of fourteen. If it is too much for the ears, "Onward and Upward with the Arts—The New Sound" by Renata Adler, in *The New Yorker,* Feb. 20, 1965, pp. 63-105, is recommended; or the reader might try scrounging around among the record shops for a song already five years old—what the vendors call a gold record (goodie but oldie)—it is "I Will Follow Him" and was sung by Little Peggy March. This song was running through the author's mind during the writing of *Miss Post's English Assignment,* and Elizabeth Browning's two lines were his attempt to capture its spirit.

talked instead, of God, of fellowship and sacrifice, the secret sympathy, or of anything except the love that they are warned by their troubadours never to betray.

Now we see that this exception to the practical mode does not hold; clearly even with *Miss Post's English Assignment* our respondents were being practical, and in exactly the same way that they had been practical before. Consider, for instance, the persons whom they had encountered in other episodes. Among them there was Mr. Clarke, the social studies teacher. He might just as well have been a coach or a typing instructor. What was important was that he was a teacher, and in framing a solution what had to be considered was his teacherness. Thus, an often favored choice for Episode I was to turn the miscreant over to the principal for disposition (Card [4]), even though it was readily acknowledged that the principal had little to offer in the way of effective punishment—maybe a scolding, a detention or two, and that was that; but the principal's probable ineffectualness hardly mattered to our respondents. They supported Card (4) simply because Mr. Clarke was a classroom teacher, not an expert on discipline or psychological problems; his job was to teach, not to punish. The disciplinary authorities had been hired by the school for the latter purpose.

Often, our subjects were even a bit concerned for Mr. Clarke, should he undertake to punish Johnny. They worried that he might get into trouble for this. In solving Episode I they focused on the teacher *qua* teacher, not on the man, Clarke. Their concern was that he act like a teacher, not out of indignation nor with indifference. For this reason they were most emphatic that he not walk out of the washroom, as was suggested on Card (9). He should act, instead, they insisted, like a teacher acts and do his bureaucratic duty as he ought.

Again, with Coach Regan in Episode II, the respondents were, above all things, practical. With no easy out, they were often left perplexed. Yet, they remonstrated, could a coach—Mr. Regan's role—ever think of anything except winning? The answer was an emphatic no. Our subjects could not believe that a coach might be concerned about the larger implications of his function.

For Episode IV, there was the King, possibly an enlightened king. Poor King, think how meager were his chances of ever meeting a spirited American youth, since for our respondents the important thing was to make a good impression on him. Again, as it was teacher *qua* teacher, not Mr. Clarke, and coach *qua* coach, not Mr. Regan, so it was king *qua* king, whatever that might be—not a pleasant, sophisticated man of the world looking forward to a lively afternoon's talk with several bright, possibly edgy young people. Imagine Shaw's King Magnus sentenced for an afternoon to association with the likes of Karen Clarke. It must be a cruel fate to be a king on a visit to the land of the free and the home of the brave if this is all that can be offered—a pseudo-event.

Even Mr. Blakely was handled in these same polite, impersonal, highly pragmatic terms, despite the fact that it is possible to become angry with him if one reads carefully enough. Righteous indignation may have its place, but not when practical matters are being considered—not for our subjects any more than for Mr. Clarke. Mr. Blakely was doing his job, wasn't he, and in a world as interdependent as ours the Mr. Blakelys are necessary; they keep things in place.

Alan's parents also had their duty. They, however, did not seem to recognize the limits of parenthood and insisted on butting in where they didn't belong. That they showed concern for their wayward son was commendable. That they insisted on doing something about their concern was outrageous—a violation of their proper function. Their duty was to be parents *qua* parents, to recognize the legitimacy of Mr. Blakely's authority and to support it, not to be Mr. and Mrs. Slade, troublemakers (and neurotic troublemakers at that). Didn't the episode disclose that they knew so little of how to run their own lives that they needed a psychiatrist to keep their marriage together? Such effrontery, to question Mr. Blakely's judgment. With parents like the Slades, who can't seem to understand, it was no wonder poor Alan was having his difficulties.

Now, back to Miss Post. For our respondents there could be no significance in Elsie Post the person—warm, understanding, competent, and wise; there was only the teacher *qua* teacher to contend with. The solution for the practical-minded was to treat the assignment as an assignment to be done for a teacher, an *any* teacher. That this teacher might be a person of sensitivity was only a chance one took with the odds, just as it was only a chance that the King might actually have enjoyed spending afternoons with bright and lively young people, or that Mr. Clarke might have been a relatively peaceful fellow and that he was only looking for a quiet place for a smoke himself. Disregarding such odd chances, practical respondents thought in terms of normal expectations and interpreted each episode accordingly. Mr. Clarke *qua* teacher was expected to make trouble. In the same way, as Miss Post was a teacher the sensible thing was to give her the kind of responses that would impress her. Cards (2), (3), and (6), which when not dealing in pious generality dealt with the gentle proper spirit of love, were the logical choices. Cards (5), (9), and (4) were too personal, too racy, too sardonic, and had to be rejected. No teacher *qua* teacher could be expected to think of them as appropriate love poems for a high school English class.

So much for Miss Post herself and the practical matter at hand. We were wrong in thinking that sentimentalism, which simply seemed sloppiness to us, was somehow impractical. For the specific situation in Episode V it was entirely right. Our error was in assuming that the description of Miss Post would be taken seriously.

There are, however, larger questions founded on this "pragmatism." Jean and Brenda and Sharon had tried to do what was right. There was no vile cynicism in their responses, no "give the old bag what she wants and the hell with it" attitude. Fundamentally, they are very good girls, responding as best they can to an assignment. How well do they succeed in their attempt?

Of Mrs. Browning's two lines, Jean said they left her "off, blank." All right, this was simply a matter of taste. But then she went on, "It seems very cold." This is different; it is a criticism and an incorrect one, too. Sir Walter Scott's love is cold, abstract, something alien to man. But not Elizabeth Barrett's. Hers is direct, fierce, simple, anything but cold. That wasn't all, though, for then, and with a bit of a curl to her lip, Jean concluded, "It wouldn't mean anything to me if I were to read it in a book." Brenda, for her part, is snide, even a bit sarcastic. "It was supposed to be about love," she says. And Sharon is peevish, "There are silent types of love, too, I think."

These are only three of many similar responses. What they have in common is a rejection of these two lines and, further, resentful

feelings about them. Each girl, in her own way, is sour and negative. Each does more than simply disagree with the sentiments expressed in the poem: each feels the need to condemn. Technically,
such condemnation was unnecessary, even superfluous. All that
was needed to fulfill the assignment was a simple explanation as to
why the Browning excerpt did not depict love, as such. Since such a
simple explanation was not easy to come by, the girls drifted off,
instead, into obloquy.

Even more striking are the comments of a Caddo youth named
Charles regarding Card (9)—Matthew Arnold's "Dover Beach."
Charles stands about midway in the sample, and in his stance em-
braces conventionalism and transforms it into a set of principles.
He enjoys a certain toughness, also. Due to this pose, his language
is much richer than is common. Of "Dover Beach," which he
places Poor, he said,

> It wasn't down to earth. This guy's in a world of dreams. . . .
> When you think you really love somebody you gotta start
> thinking in terms of, like you get married and you gotta think
> in terms not of dream worlds but realistic dollars and cents
> and things like that. . . . You're gonna be living with this
> woman for the rest of our life and it's gonna be problems and
> everything. . . . Maybe in high school you go out with girls
> and stuff, you live in a dream world, but not when you really
> love somebody.

Charles derogates the vital love. He also plays off against it the
gentle love and its co-conspirator, marriage. They are the source of
the need for establishing the practical mode and must be respected.
He has nothing but contempt for the "shallowness" of Matthew
Arnold or for the childish ways of youth. In a word, Charles expresses a quality akin to ressentiment and directs it against the vital
love and also against those who stand, symbolically, for it.

While less vigorous, Jean and Brenda and Sharon express a similar antipathy to the vital love. Is this ressentiment? It may be. In
any case it brings to mind certain responses from *The King's Visit.*
In our subjects' discussion of the episode, Scott Cowen and Johnny
Adams were not simply rejected. Again and again our subjects
were also moved to condemn them. Both boys were described as

being willful and difficult. The respondents found it repugnant that the two youths refused to accept conventions of dress and, further, that Scott argued in class. Johnny and Scott were constantly criticized for being "underachievers," and throughout, their self-indulgence was treated as if it were some kind of betrayal. The Combo, whose members had many estimable qualities, suffered a different but not unrelated fate. They were ignored entirely, despite clear evidence of their many-sided excellence. On inquiry, we found no reason to connect this indifference to the Negro-ness of Joe White. It was simply that they were too gamey for the taste of our respondents. Thus, where Scott and Johnny were denigrated, the Combo was denied. Again, this is very like ressentiment.

Twice, then, we have found a quality akin to ressentiment in the responses of our student subjects. And in the comments of Charles, this quality was linked directly to his advocacy of the practical attitude. What does this mean?

We did not begin this study with the intention of proving that our student subjects are ressentient, but rather that the presses they experience in school are to some degree infected with ressentiment and that the net result of this infection is to stultify them. On the other hand, while we have uncovered evidence of widespread infection in the schools, we found constant difficulties with attributing ressentiment to school presses per se. The infecting is not so much by the procedures and prescriptions of the institution itself as it is by persons acting in concrete situations. Now we find in the subjects themselves evidence of qualities much like the ressentiment we had looked for in the schools. We have also identified certain values towards which the students direct their derogation. One of these is the vital love, the very love, we argue, that the respondents themselves embrace when they are at home or elsewhere—any place, that is, where they can afford to be comfortable. The other target of contempt is those classmates who are perceived to be willful, arrogant, gifted, and uneven in their performance—or, in effect, those who are engaged in seeking experience, and through it, identity; those who are most adolescent in their mode of being.

It now appears that the lies we encountered before were not so innocent. The vital love that was derogated in school is also that which is aggressive, direct, exciting, and personal in its expressiveness—in a word, it is also adolescent. In it we can recognize the fidelity of Erik Erikson discussed in "Youth: Fidelity and Diversity," [4] both in the sonnet and in the intense devotion to passionate love in rock and roll. As Scott and Johnny are adolescent, this love is also adolescent, and together they constitute the object of the denigrating ressentiment-like animus.

In formulating ressentiment in competitive terms exclusively, that is, between persons, Scheler overlooked the phenomenon we find revealed here. To him, the enemy is always a different ego. The Other, too strong to be overcome, stands in the way of the impotent One. Yet, when One is impotent and shrinks in the face of danger, One has not one, but two enemies: for the attacker outside and the weakness inside are both real. They conspire together to destroy the affirming ego, to defeat revenge. Ressentiment is as much the result of this weakness in one's own self as it is of the strength of the Other.

What we have found in our young people is a quality akin to ressentiment, yet turned inward, at their own vitality. To do this, however, the enemy has to be objectified. The adolescent that is in each of these young people is detached and made the object of their obloquy. The ressentient attack on Johnny (or, more accurately, the attack on the objectified Johnny—the nasty beatnik) and the attack on the vital love (love expressed directly) are together a self-inflicted wound; they constitute ressentiment of a sort directed by the young people against their own claim to youthfulness.

In the course of this examination of responses to *Miss Post's English Assignment* we have found in our student respondents a self-concern about their youthfulness and vitality. Tolerated under certain circumstances—such as at home (sometimes), with the crowd, at the game—but rarely in school, this young vitality is sufficiently threatening so as to have incurred a dreadful animus. In consequence, every coarse-grained occasion associated with school is tempered, managed, objectified, and stereotyped while the odd, the raw, the special, the indignant are dispossessed of a sinfulness associated with their youth.

Miss Svensen's testimony in Chapter II suggests that the young

[4] From *The Challenge of Youth*. See our discussion in Chapter I, pp. 6–7.

are caught up in a Protestant ethic, one that is certainly mundane but formidable and demanding, nevertheless. The demand it makes is that they suppress their vigor, that they "manage their tension," that they surrender their youth. This they must do for a practical purpose. Otherwise, they say, they will sink into iniquity, they will become like Johnny Barto. Barto himself, they feel, is contaminating and should be removed. Other less pernicious personifications of the sinful nature of youth, such as Johnny Adams and Alan Slade, should be corrected. Else all—because all are in some degree Alan and Johnny—all stand to lose their opportunity to enter that obscure state of bliss that is to be theirs in the heavenly city of gold. We must now enquire about that city and its exacting god.

Chapter X

THE TEACHERS' POINT OF VIEW

LET US ASSUME that an important lesson is learned in school, and let us then return to Hartsburgh, where, we remember, the Best Thing for one young man was,

> The best thing that ever happened to me was when I began to understand why I am here. I started seeing the teacher's point of view which for years I had always been against. I also began to realize the true meaning of life.

As irony does not characterize high school students, this young man probably means what he says. Similar statements from other respondents and other schools also testify to the widespread popularity of this position. What, then, is this "teacher's point of view" that students have learned to accept?

On turning to the teachers' responses, we again encounter a derogation of the vital love. Item (46) on the F-N R Index states, "If a boy and a girl go steady here, the chances are that they are really in love." Unpopular with the students, it is even more so with the teachers. A massive 97 percent of the teachers scored this item as false. In framing this item we had intended to associate going steady with the vital love, implying that serious love is as possible for modern young people as it was for Romeo and Juliet. Both teachers and students as respondents disagreed emphatically and thereby cooperated in dissolving the joys of young life as they denied the possibility of love.

Second, and more important, is the teachers' response to questions about equalitarianism. They affirm, at better than 80 percent, that "A basic principle of the way this school is supposed to be run is that everybody gets equal treatment no matter who he is" and that "When a class here is discussing a problem, the teachers think the most important thing is to have all possible points of view represented." [1] Corroborating evidence of this affirmation is offered by *The LeMoyen Dance*. For that episode teachers chose Card (6) as their most popular comment. When compared with the student response by means of a Chi-square test of significance, the computed variance estimate for the card exceeded the 1 percent level and probably the .1 percent level. That is, the teachers not only liked the card but they also liked the card *very* much better than did the students. The card reads,

Everything the school sponsors is a part of the educational program and should be open to all. It is good for the Student Council to have the experience of running the dance, as this helps them to learn to be responsible. But they must not be permitted to turn public education into an exclusive social affair.

Equalitarianism, then, receives strong support from the teachers in both Phase I and Phase II testing. For example, in discussing Card (6) an English teacher said,

. . . if the dance is part of the educational program and, I believe it is, it should be open to all. I think the Student Council should have experience in running the dance because I think this does teach responsibility, but of course, at the same time it shouldn't be too exclusive a social affair, and they do need some help and guidance.

Far more extended and carefully thought through are the comments of counselor John Burns in supporting his choice of this Card (6),

BURNS: I believe that the Student Council must learn to stand on its own two feet. And that the only way we will do this is by giving the youngsters the responsibility for planning and carry-

[1] Items (56) and (26).

ing out these dances. The Student Council must also learn, as
the card says, that when a thing, . . . a curricular activity, is
open to the entire student body, they cannot discriminate in
any way, whether it be financially, scholastically, or in any
other manner.

After a comment by the interviewer to the effect that this was a
very significant value for the school to teach, Burns continued,

BURNS: I feel that the Student Council, through adequate
guidance and adequate leadership, must come to realize that
they must adopt a set of values which will help in running the
school. . . . And that in adopting these values they must understand that the school is open to everybody.
INTERVIEWER: But what then happens to the people whose
values are different from those that the school has adopted?
BURNS: Well, it's a question that requires a little thought. Of
course we—we assume that the values of the majority of the
school, or that the Student Council, which represents the majority of the school, will adopt . . . are those best suited for
the school. . . . And that through education, and through
observation, the people who do not have similar values must
slowly adopt the values of the majority of the school, if they
are to fit into the school.
INTERVIEWER: And this would be desirable?
BURNS: I think in this case, this would be desirable. Yes.

Grounding their argument on an appeal to egalitarianism, the
teachers accept majority rule as a principle. They seek to establish
a consensus through encouraging their charges to be responsible
toward the authority embodied in the school. They appeal to equality as a justification for the school's necessary procedures. To help
their young people and guide them toward an acceptance of what
they deem is best, the teachers and administrators plan carefully
and recommend to their charges that they do likewise. The planning is also used to reduce and control the tensions attendant on
youthfulness. This, in sum, is the teachers' point of view.

As such, it is very much like the students' point of view, only
more so—more self-contained, more cleanly delineated, more thoroughly reified, and what some would term more mature. The ster-

eotypical thinking encountered in our earlier discussion of practicality recurs, with the prime object of concern now the good of all *qua* all. To the teachers the dance is most valuable when it is a learning experience for the students. The animadversion of adolescent ways also continues, and responsibility implies that the young people "shape up," stop their silliness, and set about being practical. Underlying all this is egalitarianism—a dominating moral imperative. The central importance of principled equalitarianism as a source of teacher values, and even of student values, can hardly be overstated. In consideration of its salience both for students and for teachers let us look into this equality matter more closely.

In the form of equal justice before the law, equalitarianism is certainly an excellent principle, and one to be recommended. For, whatever else it may be, established law is an imposition on individuality backed by force, and impartiality in its administration is necessary in order to prevent the law from becoming a privileged instrument and, as such, a threat to freedom and to integrity. Our respondents, however, do not seem to have equal *justice* in mind when they stress equality, for over 75 percent of the students and teachers *disagree* with the statement, "Most students' misbehavior here is handled informally, but students who insist on a formal hearing often win their cases." Results are mixed on two other items relating to justice, but hardly encouraging. Fifty-nine percent of the students feel, "If a teacher or administrator accuses a student of misbehavior here, there isn't much he can do to defend himself." On the other hand, 75 percent of the teachers report that they think the opposite true. Finally, students are 50-50 on the statement, "A student who gets on anybody's black list here has a pretty hard time; it practically takes a lawyer to get him off." Again, the teachers take exception; only one third of them agree with the statement. While these results may be contradictory, they still do not encourage belief in the interpretation that it is civil liberties the teachers have in mind when they stress equality.[2]

More certainly, it is equality of opportunity that they are thinking about, an equality based on access to an idealized position. In substance, according to this way of thinking, no one is entitled to special consideration. Formally, such equality exists in contradis-

[2] Items (38), (52), and (42).

tinction to privilege. Life is not properly a handicap race with the big, strong fellow assigned a hundred-yard lead over the scrawny one simply because he can bulldoze the judges. Nor, theoretically, should pity allow the scrawny one an advantage over his more generously endowed opponent. Differences are not supposed to count, and when both start the race with an equal opportunity to win, their differences should assert themselves in the race, not in the conditions establishing the race. Accordingly, in the name of fairness to all, the rules of the race for grades, for promotion, for graduation are carefully drawn. Each treated exactly like his fellows is given his chance to win.

The trouble is, though—and this is a serious matter—education is not a race, much as those in charge might like to think it so. It is, instead, an act of care, an effort on the part of the community to nurture its youth so that they can develop their full powers.

In its essence the equality principle—conceived of as a race among equals with equal access to fair treatment—is a conscious act of negation. It is appropriate for a track meet. At a race the judges ignore the special characteristics of the runners—that one has a charming manner, that another is an excellent student, and that the third is handsome, and so forth. Instead, impassive in the face of all this variety, they concentrate on the business at hand. They watch the finish line and are alert for infractions of the established rules. Their concern is to determine the winner from among those who are entered in the race. The runners have their coaches, whose job it is to treat them in their wholeness, who know their talents and deficiencies, and who seek to strengthen them in mind and in body. The judges choose the winner, and choose, we hope, fairly, having provided each runner an equal opportunity to excel; the coaches care for the runners and help them to fulfill themselves.

Education, we say, is not this; it is instead an act of care. It is also an act of faith.[3] It is a promise to another person and is com-

[3] Erich Fromm reminds us that "the root of the word education is e-ducere, literally, to lead forth, or to bring out something which is potentially present." While this definition is also alienated—the word "something" implies "thingness"; can we say that the dental technician or the dog catcher is already present in the newborn child—it does about as well as words can do. See Fromm, *Man for Himself* (New York: Holt, Rinehart & Winston, 1947), p. 207.

parable to the coaching function, not the judging function. Coaching, however, is narrow in its implications; education encompasses it and much more. The educator must have faith in each of his charges, and he must care about their reaching and growing. Care also demands that he work directly with persons pledged to his care in their "eachness," not as generalities. His task is to cultivate, to nourish; and it is a transforming function. It is expensive and demanding and committed to liberty. The equality principle, which has real merit when applied in appropriate situations, refers to judging, not to coaching. As negation, it cannot allow care to interfere and is blind to faith. Consequently, it is not a sufficient basis on which to establish education.

In fact, there is a real danger in the equality principle. Properly used this principle guarantees the fair running of the race. It functions in the immediate present and, in establishing its indifference to variety, allows a specific basis for judgment to be implemented —the crossing of the finish line, for example. In this sense its calculated passivity has great merit. Through treating the individual as an abstract generality, a systematic procedure for ascribing excellence becomes possible.

On the other hand, the equality principle can also be badly used. For instance, if all shoes for the consumer market were manufactured only in size 9C, most of us would have to do without shoes. If they were of only one design, albeit with an adequate range of sizes, there would still be a considerable measure of dissatisfaction. And, when we consider that the education of a young man or woman is far more complex than is the satisfaction of the demand for shoes, we can see where the trouble lies. There is a necessary variety in shoe manufacturing because it deals with people in terms of their particular needs. The same necessity holds for schools. Education cannot afford to be blind to variety. The danger implicit in the equality principle lies in the possibility that the variety and charm of the concrete being will be lost over the edge of "thingness." In effect, the equality principle becomes egalitarian ideology, a leveling ideal which denies individualizing significations. Indifferent to caring, the righteous ideologist judges, and in this judgment the person disappears into the abstraction.

The teacher who makes certain that everyone has an adequate

opportunity to express his ideas during recitation is operating within the limits of the equality principle. The teacher who makes a virtue of the recitation itself, ignoring, in the name of fairness to everyone, the contradictory, the factually false, or the poetic, or, in other words, the substance of the recitation, is guilty of this leveling egalitarianism. In the name of equality, intelligibility and beauty are rejected. Much the same can often be said of the individual who asserts that everyone receives equal treatment in his class. In certain contexts a student has every right to expect this of his teacher. But he also has the right to expect other forms of consideration.[4]

The equalitarian act when used is similar in form to the ressentient act. Both throw the individual out of focus and make him into an abstract generality. It is only in their intention that the two processes are different. Ressentiment is a direct aggression designed to make the object persons suffer; equalitarian is simply the easiest way to be. An equalitarian ethos, as a result, is especially susceptible to ressentiment because it constitutes a possible medium for the value transformation. In itself, though, egalitarian ideology is danger enough. With equalitarianism as the cardinal principle guiding education, whether as an expression of ressentiment or simply out of expedience, teaching will become perverted. The task of teaching grows, as we have said, out of care. It is properly rooted in what the individual can express, given his personal vitality and a rich measure of this care, and it can only be fulfilled in its object through this expression. Any decision about education that reifies the persons being educated must be taken only with great caution. Yet, this is exactly what happens when egalitarian ideology is established as the cardinal principle of education.

The great bulk of our teacher responses show acceptance of egalitarian ideology as an overriding value commitment. This they may

[4] We recognize that in talking about the teacher and the school as we have throughout this section, we too are guilty of reducing persons to abstractions. This is in contradistinction to our previous efforts. Throughout we have attempted to bring the reader into relation with the school *qua* Parma, the student *qua* Gordon Hughes, and the teacher *qua* Mr. Burns. Nevertheless, we too must be practical, and because such practicality demands abstracting, i.e., reducing problems to manageable terms, we plead guilty to the creation of stereotypes. It hurts, though.

do either out of ressentient meanness or simply because it is the practical thing to do. While we prefer that it be for the latter reason, the danger still remains—the Gordon Hugheses must sense that they are still "under wraps." For through this egalitarianism the Many are conceived as an abstracted One, an Other, named Everybody, who replaces them as separate persons, and what catering is done is done for It.

As the focus of concern shifts to Everybody it shifts away from the separate persons. It also becomes transformed. The person is characterized by lability, growing, and a capacity for fidelity. Responsive, the person can be responsible in the face of a predicament in the here and now. On the other hand the Everybody is characterized by inertness—as an abstraction, it is constant in time —and by impassivity, which means that its capacity for response other than in predetermined modes is decidedly limited. Intermittently, such as during a strike or revolt, Everybody may get out of hand, but its normal manner is normalcy.

To conclude, when the teacher ordains egalitarianism he transforms the students who came to him as persons into subscripts to an Everybody. They become only a piece of what they ought to be. And that piece is not only a simplification of the person; it also differs in its very nature, for it is inert, whereas they, as persons, are vital. The Everybody has no need for care. What it requires is legitimation, and this it receives through its ordination by authority and its acceptance as the epitome of rightness by the students. It also requires, when there are several such Everybodies and they interlock, management. To the extent, then, that the teacher negotiates the transformation of the persons into a set of subscripts to Everybody, he can devote himself to management, which is far less demanding than caring. And, we must report, the evidence indicates that the great majority of them have organized their teaching in just this way. Such is the "teachers' point of view." Let us now consider the "true meaning of life."

Chapter XI

THE TRUE MEANING
OF LIFE

EQUALITARIANISM IS only one of the many structures of alienation common to the schools we observed. Majority rule, again
worthwhile where appropriate, is another, as are the grades many
teachers give. In each case the person is canceled out, to be replaced by a figment which stands for him. For example, an "A"
student is not simply a student, but, instead, a very special student,
one who has proved himself excellent in the judgment of his
teachers. The same is true, in a less happy way, of a "D" student.
A sum of qualitative and quantitative comparisons are reduced, for
practical purposes, to a mere symbol, implying superiority, inad-
equacy, or something. And the student so tagged can expect to
carry this symbolic representation with him forever, or so it seems,
as an attribute which, with each successive grading, becomes
firmer. In such a manner the figment grade becomes the acknowledged person. The school—itself a figment composed of teachers,
administrators, students, and others, who are also figments—then
keeps itself busy dealing with these various figments and their pur-
ported needs. As a result, the bundle of figments absorbs the concern originally destined for the person. The school is thus an institution, or, as articulated in Sartre's new terminology, "an inorganic
unification of a serialized multiplicity." [1]

[1] R. D. Laing and D. G. Cooper, *Reason and Violence, A Decade
of Sartre's Philosophy, 1950-1960* (London: Tavistock Publications,
1964), p. 161. We acknowledge our indebtedness to the recent work

The relationship of student to Everybody, identified in our examination of the equality principle in Chapter X and now broadened to include a whole range of such relationships, is what Sartre calls *seriality*. Each person is a totality in himself. Yet, each person may also exist as part of a plurality of persons conceived of in terms of some object. The figment part of him that joins with his figment fellows in series is Other to the "him" in his solitude. It has an objective character, a determined future, and a determining past, and, to the extent that he (the person) commits himself to the object defining this figment part of himself (or must commit himself to it), it becomes a fragment of his destiny. In his character as figment, then—herein as student, as one of the Everybodies—he is the same as his fellows and shares with them a common fate.

To the degree that the figments are systematized, the multiplicity of organic persons is replaced by an inorganic unification—an institution. A school is such an institution. In itself it performs a necessary function, for it is through its mediation that young people are fitted to society. Only one of several such mechanisms—the most notable other being the family—the school is especially important for an industrial-bureaucratic society. This is because the school as an institution is radically alienated and alienating. The structure imposed is cleanly reified and functions on an abstract level, in the image of the society itself. In the school the points of interaction are sharply delimited and circumscribed. One encounters the teacher mainly in formalized situations. By comparison, authority figures in the family—father, mother, aunt—are encountered at many points of interaction. The teacher-student relationship is further alienated through its dependence on language and on a distinct subject matter.

Examples of alienation in school, when compared with the family, are abundant; to pursue them further will only distract. What is important to consider here is that we live in a society which has become radically institutionalized, and that, in such a society, education as an inorganic unification has a distinct virtue. It is through

of Jean-Paul Sartre for the analysis contained in this chapter and the next one. For a summary of his multi-faceted effort the reader is referred to Laing and Cooper's work. The relevant books by Sartre are cited in our bibliography.

its efforts that young people are wrenched from the arms of their parents and trained to cooperate in the bureaucratic larger world. This is a necessary act, it would seem, for we need radically alienated people for our radically alienated world.

Nevertheless, an alienated educational system, whatever its fitness, comes close to being a contradiction in terms. An institution constituted as such may be of excellent service. It can perform repetitive tasks even when these are of great complexity. Education, however, while repetitive too, connotes a special kind of repetitiveness. What is attempted is not to repeat an operation but to bring to fruition each of many growth processes. If it is to be the kind of education in which responsible persons care *about*, not just care *for*, their charges, it must recognize the variety in the person and then respond to each in terms appropriate to his uniqueness. Otherwise education is simply another form of manufacturing, and a cruel one at that.

When we ask then why there is aggressive institutionalizing in education, despite the many excellent people who love to teach and to nurture the growth of learning and even wisdom in the young, the answer is—as has been evident throughout the study—because it works. Thus, practicality appears again. Through the good offices of the institution the Many can be managed, handled, controlled, and directed along specific paths with efficiency. This can even be justified as being for their own good—the students', that is—as it prepares them for success in the world at large.

A simple example from teaching may help to demonstrate this practicality. Headquarters, the principal's office, decrees that the teacher must grade his students; otherwise, there will be no basis on which to recommend them. To grade, the teacher can either construct an objective test or assign a theme. The test is easy to correct, albeit difficult to construct—unless of course one uses canned items from the teachers' manual. It also provides what to most teachers is an acceptable basis for ranking students. On the other hand, grading themes, when one is serious about it, is an arduous task, is time-consuming, and because of the subjectivity involved always leaves the grader unsatisfied. No matter how you look at them, B minuses on two different themes never mean quite the same thing. Furthermore, the grade on a theme, when given, is subject to challenge. After all, the student may charge that the teacher has been unfair; and the teacher has no "objectivity" to fall back on.

Clearly, the objective test is practical, the theme is not. Nevertheless, and for one simple reason, the theme is far superior to the objective test as an educating instrument. On the multiple-choice test the best that the student can do is to agree perfectly with the pre-formed idea of the teacher—a thing from the teacher's mind reified through the test and identified as good, now and for a short forevermore. On the theme, however, the student can surpass the teacher. Almost always, the best theme is a surprise to the grader; often he can learn something from it. Even the worst theme, when it shocks, can also be a lesson to the teacher. On the other hand, the objective test, except in cases where it is poorly drawn, can never be a surprise, only a disappointment. Once constructed, it is an alien entity and belongs neither to the teacher nor to the student, but instead has a life of its own, and one that absorbs, in part at least, their vitality and their individuality. The student, for example, can steal the test, and with his special knowledge of its contents, take advantage of the teacher.

We find again all the elements of the pragmatism we recognized before: the act is practical in that a resolution to a present problem is achieved. A grade is given, with a minimum of pain for all concerned. An inert Other has instigated a reflex action—this time the Other is a set of correct answers, not a stereotype—and the persons involved have submitted passively to this Other. Both student and teacher accept the test as a legitimate basis for grading. The student, in his figmentizing mode, plans his study in terms of the questions he anticipates will be asked. The teacher accepts the test's judgment as if it were his own. The inert form, here the objective test, is thus a structure of what Sartre terms the *practico-inert,* an all-encompassing term.[2] Actually, the theme is too, after it has been written. It can be stolen and may be submitted by one not its author. The difference between the two assignments, however, concerns their individual relationship with the practico-inert. By assigning the theme, the teacher gives the honest student an opportu-

[2] See Wilfrid Desan, *The Marxism of Jean-Paul Sartre* (New York: Doubleday, 1965), Chapter 5.

nity to contribute a structural element to the practico-inert whereas the student facing the objective test can contribute nothing but must instead respond entirely in terms established by the teacher. The theme writer has a measure of liberty for expression. He acts. The test-taker reacts to an indifferent Other.

Institutionalizing is not always quite so innocent and passive, however. Sometimes the school decides to be meddlesome and insinuate its power into the lives of its students. Take dress regulations, for example. One might reasonably assume that the clothes a youth wears are a matter for himself, his parents, and, in cases of wrong committed, the law. Many times, though, the schools do not accept this and consider student attire very much their business. When asked why they intrude in this area, they insist that clothes are very important—almost, it seems, that they *do* make the man.

Against this, consider that young people in the fullness of their vitality are also at their most beautiful. With them clothes can readily be an expression of their persons. That is, the clothes they wear can accentuate the beauty that is theirs. In so doing, clothes may also help to make them prideful, idiosyncratic, exciting, selfish, and sexy. Allowed expression, such attitudes can encourage trouble. The young people caught up in this excitement may churn about and become difficult to handle. In consequence, for practical reasons institutions regulate dress.

What can be worn is defined, of course, by the tastes of the adult institutors. To support these standards they condemn the exotic as bad taste, discourage innovation, and point out how much better conservative dress is for everybody concerned. Bad taste here is the negation of the school-defined taste which, by definition, thereby becomes good taste. Good taste is the negation of the individualized taste of the student-person. Hence, bad taste is adolescent taste. The values are adjusted to fit the situation. What is young is bad, what is old is good, and the opportunity youth has lies in showing good taste. This, then is the negation of negation.

This is not simply a matter of playing on words, for that which is negated is adolescent vitality itself. Dress regulations implement the denigration of the spirit and joy of youth fulfilled. With the negation of negation the vital values have been replaced with values derived from fear. The morality of the dress regulations is essentially negative and defensive and is based on distrust. This, of course, in its formal sense is ressentiment.

Here, the institutionalizing is aggressive. The school extends its range of control, seeking insidiously to displace adolescent values with those favoring school-defined values. This encroaching alienation is no longer automatic—a reflex response to practical concerns —but is, instead, inspired by the animus noted earlier, aggressive in intent, and aimed at youth itself.

Several negative comments by teachers about Johnny Adams serve to illustrate this point. For *The King's Visit* Johnny is next to Eric Pratt in unpopularity with teachers; thirty-one out of fifty-five would not send him as the school's representative. Eric, of course, is a "dress regulations" problem—he has style and overdresses— as is the third most unpopular choice with teachers, Scott Cowen. Nothing is said on Johnny's card about the way he dresses; however, it does say that he isn't especially "good-looking" and that most of the time "he could use a haircut and shave." The derogation of Johnny begins with dress and extends inward, to his attitude. In rejecting Johnny, an industrial arts teacher said,

> . . . usually the people draw impressions from first appearances. Unless you could change the way he dresses, and the way he looks, and the way he acts much of the time, although he might be a very intelligent person, I don't think he would be a very good impression of the school itself. You never know how a guy like this is going to act.

Dress seems especially important to teachers of commercial subjects. A woman, teaching bookkeeping, continued,

> He doesn't have enough personal pride in himself. I do not feel that a youngster has to be particularly—I mean expensively—dressed. He certainly doesn't have to be—I mean . . . thank God we're not all gifted with . . . say, builds, or voices, and so on, but the Lord tells us we should do the best with what we have.

In this statement we find pride associated with achieving the social norm, not in a personal achievement. In fact, the whole response is rancid with ressentiment. A counselor had this to say of Johnny,

Here's a person who because of his appearance, and the fact that he's difficult to get along with—he's erratic, sometimes he performs well, sometimes he doesn't—you can't count on him making the proper impression.

Johnny's alleged erratic nature is often held against him. A math teacher compared him with those he would prefer,

> . . . it strikes me that he only does things when he feels like it. He's not the kind of student that I would . . . prefer over other students who do things not only when they feel like it, but do them all the time.

The difference between the school-oriented student—in our terms, the one who allows the Other to dominate—and Johnny, who is self-absorbed, is clear in this statement. Finally, we have a science teacher who discussed Johnny with sorrow,

> Johnny Adams seems to be a thorn in my side. I think that the adolescent or the average kid today has a fairly soft time. Years ago times were hard, money was hard, and so on. . . . Today, he has his choice of styles in activities, and cars, . . . and so many of them today are sitting back and becoming beatniks, . . . and I feel that the man or the boy who has potentials, he can go further. Occasionally he can be spirited or stimulated, whatever you want to call it, to show that he can perform. However, in my estimation, a person such as this that does not perform is a waste to society.

These are not every teacher—six of the fifty-five did choose Johnny to go on the visit—but the statements above do represent the majority.

In them, we observe again the animus found so often before and, further, a stress on order, and a concern about Johnny's erratic nature. Their testimony suggests that the acceptable student is the one who does what he is supposed to do and does this all the time, or, in terms used earlier, the acceptable student is the conventional. It is he who is at home with the practico-inert. The teachers are forever practical themselves. They see the danger in Johnny's adolescent attitudes, the indecency of youth, and the need for control. Driven by the animus they have developed, they cooperate together to extend and broaden the range of control. This is the source from which spring dress regulations and, in addition, that whole paraphernalia of controls that we found scattered about in the schools —the Hartsburgh Rep, the Parma Way.

The purpose of the school, institutionalized, is to bring the young people into line. Partly a product of necessarily alienating arrangements associated with organization, this institution may also reflect accumulated animus against the youth. This animus, and the malice it encourages, is not antithetical to the institution, however, for the institution, founded on the practico-inert, itself favors passivity. Consequently, the ressentiment associated with the animus serves the institution well, in keeping with its purpose, which is to translate persons into things so that they will operate efficiently in the mechanism. In this way ressentiment performs a vital function for the institution. The institution, a larger structure of the practico-inert than the test situation, has no vitality in itself. It depends for its vigor on the vitality of its instituters. Well-socialized institutional functionaries tend to passivity, and if the system depended on them alone, things might disintegrate. The ressentient ones, however, are dynamically alienating, and thereby, through their nastiness, contribute creatively to aggressive institutionalizing. They are functionaries of the practico-inert.

The erratic nature the young people only too often display—that is, their diversity—is seen as a threat to the social order, which must be corrected while it is still correctable. That this erratic nature is also of the very essence of adolescence is not germane. Control and a practical eagerness for control dominate, and events are interpreted in their terms. In its efforts to direct youth along the proper path, the school offers its students first, a carrot—future success in the job world—and second, for encouragement, it whacks them with a stick—it keeps a file in which it systematically records their achievements and their failures. Teachers and administrators often seem to view themselves as surrogates of a warmhearted but strict world, a world that will reject those of their students who have not learned the habit of being good. In this, of course, they are often correct, the world being of much the same fabric as the school.

Nevertheless, this is not the only value that the teachers and administrators serve. To a much greater extent they are accomplices of the institution, not its masters. This we saw in the example of the test and theme. The institution—here a school—has a life force of its own. Founded on order, it demands order. In conformity with this the institution rewards those who contribute to its force—our successful science students from Chapter I—and punishes those who sin against its inflexible will—those who express the labile vitality that can exist in both young and old. Chances are that Gordon Hughes eventually will have to pay for his willful self-seeking, even in a great society like ours. Inert itself, the institution prefers people who are inert—that is, stable and predictable in terms of the Other that they are. It rewards the Everybodies. Thus we find the true meaning of life for the institution is the reverse of the old saw about the function of science: the institution and those who manage it, together seek to control, so that they can predict.

Chapter XII

FREEDOM IS WHEN
YOU GRADUATE
FROM HIGH SCHOOL

DURING AN INTERVIEW a simpleminded young man began to talk of freedom. Something didn't make sense about what he said so the interviewer asked him what he meant. The youth replied, "Freedom is when you graduate from high school!"

Most of the young people know better, of course. They have learned the value of accepting conventionality. There will always be a high school or another institution similar to it. So they learn to live with what is and what is always going to be. They know they cannot escape and try to accommodate.

They are young, though—adolescent—with tendencies toward fidelity and diversity. It is natural for them to love and hate and feel indignation, and it is not natural for them to be inert. At times, as the school demands, the students react. This is the other moment of the dialectic; it stands as antithesis to the encroaching, meddling institution and is, in turn, itself dialectical. The institution drives a wedge into the heart and spirit of each. Acceptance and refusal—yes and no—together characterize the response of the young people. Each answers with both a measure of resignation in favor of the institution's demands and a mete of resistance in honor of his own vital singularity. They are, after all, in the full bloom of their youth, no matter how often they may deny it, and they have in themselves a great strength for battle. Hence, their alienated education precipitates a crisis in alienation for them as it reaches out into their lives.

Their singular vitality is not readily downed. Like the young man who anticipates freedom, each in his own way seeks to assert his independence. We will remember that there were anomalies in everyone's Q-sort choice pattern. Milgrim and Martingale responses, for example, led us to infer that a wide variety of defensive techniques had been developed by the young people at those schools. Among them were apathy, cheating on tests, making school a joke, conning the teacher, and stupidity. We do not even dare speculate how much of the stupidity encountered is a mode of defense against the institution and its instituters. Some of the more innocent take flight; boys drop out, hoping to "make a lot of money," and girls get married as soon as they can. And there must even be a few sly ones who learn to live with alienation and use it to their own advantage, although they are especially difficult to track down.

Emancipation is not possible, however. There is no life in our world except in institutions. There may be ecstatic moments, when the screaming mobs of teen-agers, caught up in the excitement and the music, assail authority with abandon, but these are of short duration. And afterwards, there is always a demand for retribution. There is no safety in such rebellion.

Everybody—teachers, students, parents, neighbors, friends—is concerned about the sinful, antisocial ways of the young and the need for straightening them out. So they pitch in and help. The committed rebels, and let us assume that Johnny Adams is one such, are systematically shunned. The crowd of teen-agers is condemned out of hand, and there is always that faint note of derision at their childish ways. The affirming vigor of adolescent hubris is possible only when, as at Caddo, the practico-inert does not, for some reason, notice; or when the inert series has given way to a movement involving the students as individuals, as at Havencrest. At Havencrest, of course, the movement is synthetic; it was invented by the principal. Refuge, such as the home to which the youth can go in safety, also offers succor. Contrast, for example, Milgrim, where the school and the parents have different sets of values, with St. Elmo, where the school insists that the parents too must comply. The fierce spirit still burns at Milgrim. In the long run though, Everybody usually wins over the person, and this even in the friendliest circumstances, or so it seems. The student learns to accept the institution as the dominating force in his life and resigns himself to defending it. The interdependency of society demands that Mr. Blakely be supported despite any secret admiration for Alan Slade. And, as for Johnny Barto, if he insists on his contaminating ways, he must be removed from the society of good people.

We are often asked, "How do you know that your respondents are telling you the truth?" The answer is, we know that they aren't, and we also know that they are.

Miss Post helped us to smoke out their lie about themselves, to show us that they were responding in bad faith. Despite their romantic fancy, they answered us in the cant of gentle love. Miss Post made them nervous because she brought them so close to their lie, and for that reason they denied her existence. But it wasn't only Miss Post: the same process was evident elsewhere. There were those respondents, for instance, who insisted that Mr. Blakely's actions were both unprofessional and a gross invasion of privacy. This is what they affirmed when they chose Card (7) as Good on Alan Slade. Yet, several of these same students also insisted (by affirming Card 1) that Alan was lucky to have a counselor so devoted to helping him. When they did this they had told their lie. And, in our judgment, this lie arises out of their bad faith, their rejection of the institution they accept. So they tell us little stories, we, the Other, about how good they are, but with an undertone of reservation. This is their lie.

They also told the truth. In our files we have a thing—an alien entity that we have taken from them but which still is them—a pile of tapes and 10,000 pages of testimony. This, and only this, is what the young people chose to say about themselves. Without a doubt they conceived of us as the Other, and, in the mode of the practico-inert, they told us what the Other likes to hear about them—that is, of their personal propriety, of their sympathetic understanding of Other's needs, and of their recognition of Other's concern for them. They volunteered the two Johnnys, and Scott, and Alan for Other's purgatory. They befriended Mr. Clarke, who stood in danger of making a serious error, and castigated Mr. and Mrs. Slade for their unreasonableness. In all this they expressed their profound respect for the institution and their need for its good will. Intermittently throughout, the other truth—the eternal vigor of youth—erupted. But mostly, there was acceptance of their fate and resignation in the face of what they stood to lose. This was the essence of their conventionalism.

The tapes record their testimony and their social exterior, and unless they get into trouble (say, through drag-racing or an excessive indulgence in Beatlemania), their social exterior is the only truth that counts. For the alien Other that is society (Everybody again) responds only to this exterior. It takes as little notice of the whole man as is possible. The figment exteriors combined form the practico-inert. Everybody, impassive, deals only with the Everybodies in each man. In an institutionalized world the real man is the alienated figment which responds in concert with the other figments in the bundle. What exists outside the figment, what is negated, is irrelevant.

Even Johnny Adams, unkempt, is in the world of Everybody— he only has meaning in that world. His lack of a shave is a sneaky vengeance, like ressentiment, and, further, another negation of negation. If it were a matter of his having forgotten, that would be one thing, but more likely he has consciously not shaven in order to get a rise from his teachers and thereby to force them to punish him. His trick, and he knows it is a trick, is to make them notice him, even to punish him, for that reifies the recognition. It is not simply a matter of attention, either, for when he has been successful in forcing them to punish him they also punish themselves, that part of themselves that would prefer to be a slob. He demands of them thereby an even greater Otherness. This is his vengeance.

Nevertheless, his act, if correctly analyzed, is also creative. Ill-disposed as it is, it flows from Johnny himself and inserts itself into the practico-inert. It is an assertion, a new act of figmentizing, and as such it reconstitutes the institution in a minor way. Once committed, however, it will likely fall back into the practico-inert, to become another thing, controlling in itself. Johnny will have to be continuously inventive if he is to maintain his edge against the practico-inertia of the institution. We reviewed earlier how Johnny Barto was remanded to the disciplinary authorities. The institution is very experienced in de-energizing its youth. It carefully avoids meeting energy with energy, and even Mr. Clarke was not allowed his opportunity to punish imaginatively. With time, unless the vital force is very strong, or very slyly used, it will wither as the separate individuals allow themselves to be absorbed into the inorganic unification of the Other. The figments interconnect and become the self, reified, and it is this self that Everybody rewards for its social adaptability, for the responsibility it displays. Throughout the interviews the young people demonstrated again and again how completely they had allowed the Other to absorb them and to turn them against the adolescent in themselves. This then became the true meaning of life that Gordon Hughes refused to understand: that he must become submissive before the alienating society. Nevertheless, he probably will submit eventually. Then one can imagine how, in years hence, he may look back with some nostalgia to the old days. The vigor will have become only a memory of lost excitement. And then, nostalgia over and the business of the day at hand, he will set about, practically, at eradicating the vigor of the children of his day and, in the process, seek to solicit the assistance of the young themselves in their own subornation.

This is extreme, intentionally extreme, to make the point, and it is not fair to Gordon Hughes, who is trying, and trying hard to will himself. It is also unfair to many of the teachers whom we met. The institutions of education can have their positive moments as well as their negative ones. Many fine people teach much that is worthwhile, and with care, too.

For the most part, however, we have been concerned with the negative moment and its effect on our youth. Both by a logical process implicit in the very nature of an institution—described analogically through the example of the test versus the theme—and in response to the derogation of adolescence—examined through a consideration of dress regulations and the reasons why there are such—we find in the educational institution a necessary tendency to insinuate itself into the lives of the young. Through this insinuation those who participate in the institution, including faculty as well as students, will find their lives being absorbed into the practico-inert. As a result of this absorption the living process becomes both threatening and sterile. In response, the young people (the faculty, too, without a doubt), to survive, evince bad faith. In part this protects them. But, as time goes on, the affirmation of what is hurting them in their very vitals creates an abominable reaction. They find it practical to derogate in themselves the adolescent vitality that threatens their success in the institution. And as it persists, this derogation, originally only camouflage, eats its way into their character and erodes the life-affirming spirit. It becomes an attribute of their being. In consequence, the alienation before which they are impotent precipitates ressentiment in them, too.

To be free of this, in a way to graduate from high school for good, is what we think Gordon Hughes really wanted. But, if we are correct, he cannot be free of the ressentiment-infected, alienating institution. All that he can do is try to the best of his ability to avoid the contaminating influence of the socializing agencies, and if he succeeds in this it will probably be only at great cost to himself.

Sputnik was still flying when we first met the prototype of Johnny Adams. As a freshman he had been considered brilliant and was potentially a creative scientist. By his junior year, however, he had become elusive, was often afflicted with ennui, and insisted on being conscientiously impractical. Yet, he, like Gordon Hughes, was a thoughtful and imaginative young man, a pleasure to know. Because we were interested in what might have happened to him we undertook the study, discussed in Chapter I, of science dropouts in college.

While interviewing for that study we met many prototypes of Karen Clarke, male as well as female but all essentially conventionals like Karen. They were able to tolerate boredom. Although attending college, they were also, in a sense, still in high school and did not know what freedom was. We could not see Karen as making a creative contribution unless, somehow, she were to recapture her initiative. And it looked as if this could only be done at the expense of becoming like Johnny, a choice demanding that she take a chance with straying. Knowing that the system has short shrift for its prodigal sons, and that she had been well-conditioned, we took little comfort in this hope. Rebellion was not her style, and if she were to rebel it would only be at great cost to her and her society.

On completion of the dropout study we were not satisfied that we had done much more than to delineate a problem. Both Karen and Johnny seemed flawed to us and unlikely to find a fully satisfying life. As we were concerned about them and what had happened to them, we undertook the present study, in order to examine whether there might be something pernicious in experience that had operated to make them the way they were. We selected ressentiment to study for the reasons mentioned in Chapter II. Our try at nailing down this elusive process, while not altogether successful, has proved enlightening, even horrifying. It now seems, however, that ressentiment is only part of the story. Alienation itself, as a necessary accommodation to the practico-inert, presents serious obstacles to growth in vigor that are unavoidable. In response to the encroachments of the practico-inert a crisis in alienation develops for each. In the face of this crisis the polar alternatives are absorption into the practico-inert—Karen's alternative—or retreat into solitude—Johnny's alternative. Ressentiment's main role is to invigorate the encroaching institution and thereby to exacerbate the crisis.

The schools play their part in this dynamic process. Established to train youth for an adult world, they give our young people their primary experience with institutions. In this, our evidence suggests, they are guided by a general intention to serve society's purposes. They have also absorbed a major part of the parental role. As a result of the school's institutionalizing efforts, our Gordon Hughes, our Johnny Bartos, our Alan Slades and their friends, in their individuality and in their variety, are all being shaped, inexorably, and in a sense, unconsciously, for the practical world of Everybody. The crisis in alienation represents their efforts to will themselves despite the power of this encroaching practico-inert. But in a world of systems, escape is impossible, and eventually each must make his peace with society. In this sense, as they make their peace . . . for better or for worse . . . they become society's children.

APPENDICES

Appendix A

PHASE I TESTING

PART I: THE RESSENTIMENT INDEX

[PHASE I testing, which sought to measure the intensity of ressentiment in the nine schools, consisted of: (1) the ressentiment index, (2) the Best Thing-Worst Thing Test, in which the respondent was given two blank sheets of paper and asked to write the best thing that had ever happened to him in high school and the worst thing, and (3) the Non-Verbal Perception Test. In answering the ressentiment index, the respondent was asked to answer true if he thought the statement generally true or characteristic of his high school, that is, something which occurs or might occur, or an example of the way people tend to feel or act. The respondent was asked to answer false if he thought the statement was not characteristic of his high school. At the beginning of the testing session the respondent was given an examination booklet containing all of the instruments.

The Friedenberg-Nordstrom Ressentiment Index begins on page two of the examination booklet. In reproducing it here, we include the statement itself and the letter "T" or "F," denoting whether the item is keyed true-as-ressentiment or false-as-ressentiment. Following each statement we have reported the results, by school, from student respondents and from teacher respondents. For students, the figure given is the percentage of those answering according to the ressentiment key. The actual number of students responding from each school approximates 100. For teachers, the numbers given is the actual number of teachers responding according to the ressentiment key. A grand average for students from all schools and another for teachers are included for each item. In cases where the student response at a school differs significantly from the grand average for all schools, such significance is designated by an asterisk (*) if the difference is at the 5 percent level of significance and a dagger (†) if at the 1 percent level. Such levels of significance are computed by a Chi-square test of significance.

In reporting results for the F-N R Index, we give the schools in the order in which they were discussed. As student responses (S) are in percentages, N for students equals 100. For teachers (T), N differs from school to school. For Parma, $N = 7$; for Hartsburgh, $N = 8$; for Milgrim, $N = 5$; for Martingale, $N = 6$; for Caddo, $N = 7$; for Delphi, $N = 6$; for Havencrest, $N = 6$; for Ipswich, $N = 6$; for St. Elmo, $N = 6$; for a total, altogether, of fifty-seven teachers participating in Phase I of the testing. GAAS refers to Grand Average All Schools.]

	Parma	Hartsburgh	Milgrim	Martingale	Caddo	Delphi	Havencrest	Ipswich	St. Elmo	GAAS
1. Students here know that in science the easiest way to solve a problem is usually the best way. Key F										
S	65	58	54	50	49	71†	55	60	39†	55.4
T	2	7	4	4	6	3	5	3	3	65.0
2. The student paper here is pretty careful not to print anything too critical of the faculty or administration. Key T										
S	92†	72	76	76	81	76	73	65*	76	75.7
T	6	7	3	6	7	5	2	1	5	73.6
3. When they don't know the answers and you do, the other students here expect you to help them, such as, when taking a test, by giving them a chance to see your paper. Key T										
S	39	64†	73†	72†	76†	25†	22†	5†	26†	44.0
T	0	3	3	5	2	0	0	0	0	22.8
4. Students here are left pretty well to themselves to do what seems reasonable to them in their clubs and activities. Key F										
S	41*	46†	32	31	31	16†	20†	34	37	31.6
T	3	3	3	5	4	3	3	3	3	52.6
5. The way to get good marks here is to tell the teachers what they want to hear. Key T										
S	31	43	50†	37	35	37	34	36	35	37.2
T	1	3	0	3	5	2	1	0	4	33.3

	Parma	Hartsburgh	Milgrim	Martingale	Caddo	Delphi	Havencrest	Ipswich	St. Elmo	GAAS

6. The main thing that keeps initiations from getting too rough around here is that the members and pledges really like one another; the pledges get paddled and roughed up just enough to make them feel at home. Key F

	Parma	Hartsburgh	Milgrim	Martingale	Caddo	Delphi	Havencrest	Ipswich	St. Elmo	GAAS
S	62	75†	54	71*	34†	38†	65	87†	69	61.0
T	5	8	4	6	5	4	4	6	4	80.7

7. Teachers are always on the alert to make certain that there is no cheating around here. Key T

	Parma	Hartsburgh	Milgrim	Martingale	Caddo	Delphi	Havencrest	Ipswich	St. Elmo	GAAS
S	70	56	58	65	72	59	66	70	67	64.4
T	6	5	3	5	4	3	5	5	5	72.0

8. The faculty here make you feel like they take an interest in students and are there to help if you need them, but they generally leave you alone until asked. Key F

	Parma	Hartsburgh	Milgrim	Martingale	Caddo	Delphi	Havencrest	Ipswich	St. Elmo	GAAS
S	18	18	32*	43†	29	12*	9†	21	21	22.3
T	1	0	3	2	2	1	1	3	4	29.8

9. What students here like about biology is that a lot of good off-color jokes can be told in class without anyone being the wiser. Key T

	Parma	Hartsburgh	Milgrim	Martingale	Caddo	Delphi	Havencrest	Ipswich	St. Elmo	GAAS
S	18	27	35†	43†	14*	16	18	18	15	22.1
T	0	0	0	2	0	0	0	0	1	5.3

10. Teachers here try to be nice if students contradict them, but you can tell that they don't really like it. Key T

	Parma	Hartsburgh	Milgrim	Martingale	Caddo	Delphi	Havencrest	Ipswich	St. Elmo	GAAS
S	56	58	57	60	58	47	44	48	43	51.8
T	6	5	4	2	4	5	2	4	5	65.0

11. The best thing about courses in shop and homemaking is that they teach you how to enjoy working with your hands. Key F

S	19*	23	19*	18†	22	13†	29	66†	68†	30.4
T	4	4	1	0	2	1	5	5	3	43.9

12. You can wear anything you want to school here as long as it is decent. Key F

S	43†	46*	52	32†	36†	54	61	86†	94†	55.8
T	5	3	5	6	6	4	6	5	6	80.7

13. In answering essay questions the best thing to do is to put down everything you can think of that might just possibly bear on the question. You can't write too much. Key T

S	37	47	51	51	47	38	45	37	39	43.4
T	3	4	0	0	2	0	1	0	3	22.8

14. The main thing that determines who is in what cliques in this school is whether the members like one another. Key F

S	31	24*	26	41	30	22*	55†	47†	31	33.7
T	1	1	1	1	1	2	4	1	2	24.6

15. The teachers who have a good line, who know the latest jokes, and who always manage to make the class hour a lot of fun are the ones the students here like best. Key T

S	73	80	89†	84*	83	77	70	46†	75	74.6
T	0	6	2	1	4	1	1	0	1	28.1

16. The school takes the position that students are too young to get too involved with one another. Key T

S	58*	60*	73†	23†	64†	46	49	51	14†	47.8
T	3	4	1	2	0	3	1	1	1	28.1

	Parma	Hartsburgh	Milgrim	Martingale	Caddo	Delphi	Havencrest	Ipswich	St. Elmo	GAAS
17. Students here learn that the greatest thing about Abraham Lincoln was that he freed the slaves. Key T										
S	36	33	52†	65†	31	26	20†	25	21†	34.2
T	0	1	2	2	2	1	0	1	1	17.6
18. The student newspaper here is pretty careful not to report things in such a way that they might make trouble for the school with other people. Key T										
S	96†	86	80	83	96†	90	84	74†	80	84.5
T	5	8	4	5	5	5	3	2	5	73.6
19. The good teachers here wouldn't expect a student to tell on a friend who he knows is breaking the rules. Key F										
S	76†	61	65	52	47*	63	66	55	44†	58.4
T	6	3	3	6	4	5	4	0	2	58.0
20. A club here can invite any speaker it wants to hear, to give a talk at school. Key F										
S	39	50*	35	37	36	24†	32	48	60†	39.8
T	5	5	5	3	4	2	0	3	5	56.1
21. Students here are discouraged from using their own opinions when answering essay questions. Key T										
S	22	26	33†	28	20	13	19	8†	13	19.9
T	0	0	0	0	0	0	0	0	2	3.5
22. When it is really hot our basketball team is a beautiful thing to watch. Key F										
S	19†	26	62†	21*	54†	25	48†	28	19†	32.8
T	0	0	2	1	3	2	3	2	0	22.8

23. Good teachers are the ones who are good to students. They're understanding people who know that teen-agers have lots of troubles and they try to help them all they can. Key T

S	82	84	82	85	90	82	84	74*	89	83.0
T	6	8	2	5	7	5	3	3	5	77.1

24. Some of the most successful students around here are really brilliant. Key F

S	42	41	49	68†	44	41	38	36	28†	42.8
T	3	4	3	6	6	1	3	2	1	51.0

25. Students here often feel like they are butting their heads against a stone wall. Key T

S	54	55	67†	50	41*	45	41*	74†	49	52.3
T	0	5	4	5	3	1	0	2	4	42.2

26. When a class here is discussing a problem, the teachers think the most important thing is to have all possible points of view represented. Key T

S	89	91	86	87	91	93	90	87	88	88.7
T	6	6	5	5	7	6	5	5	3	84.2

27. Some of the librarians here try so hard to be helpful they get to be a pain in the neck. Key T

S	13†	16†	40*	70†	19*	17†	26	37	20	28.8
T	2	3	0	4	1	1	1	0	1	22.8

28. The school doesn't expect students to wear expensive clothes, but they do have to be neat and clean. Clothes that are too sporty or sexy are "out." Key T

S	81	76†	91	79	85	88	92	83	97†	85.4
T	7	7	4	6	7	6	5	5	5	91.4

	Parma	Hartsburgh	Milgrim	Martingale	Caddo	Delphi	Havencrest	Ipswich	St. Elmo	GAAS
29. A lot of teachers here use grades as a way of getting back at students. Key T										
S	14*	31	39†	44†	29	24	14*	15*	16*	24.9
T	1	3	4	1	2	1	0	0	0	21.1
30. About all that means anything to kids in this school is having a good time. Key T										
S	16	34*	49†	46†	26	15*	13†	12†	10†	24.2
T	1	1	2	2	2	0	0	1	0	15.8
31. Many teachers take pride in the tremendous amount of homework they give. Key T										
S	27	28	56†	57†	32	35	31	26	20†	34.5
T	0	3	3	1	0	0	0	2	4	22.8
32. Discrimination is not permitted here. The school insists that every club try to include at least one member from every possible minority group. Key T										
S	43	42	56	71†	55	40	41	42	55	48.9
T	3	3	3	3	3	0	2	3	5	47.4
33. Students here learn that short story writers can make a lot of money if they sell their stories to the right magazines. Key T										
S	28	27	39	52†	34	44*	33	11†	25	32.6
T	1	3	1	1	2	0	1	3	0	21.1

34. The school paper is pretty free here; any problems it leads to get thrashed out informally without too many hard feelings.   Key F

S	54	52	41	49	41	24†	52	64†	58*	47.7
T	4	5	3	3	4	0	4	1	4	49.2

35. Our librarians are very good at finding books for you that are really worth reading.   Key F

S	32	18	44†	17*	8†	26	42†	31	24	26.3
T	0	1	1	0	0	3	1	0	1	12.3

36. A girl who went too far here and got into trouble would be suspended or expelled.   Key T

S	84	77	88	83	81	90*	85	94†	61†	82.3
T	7	5	4	5	5	4	3	6	4	73.6

37. Even true/false tests here make you think.   Key T

S	3	3	7	6	2	4	4	0	3.7
T	1	1	1	2	0	4	0	1	15.8

38. Most students' misbehavior here is handled informally, but students who insist on a formal hearing often win their their cases.   Key F

S	79	73	74	79	76	71	75	80	73	75.1
T	5	5	4	5	6	6	5	5	4	79.0

39. Some teachers surprise you by getting you interested in subjects you'd never really thought much about before.   Key F

S	13	10	10	21†	9	17	9	8	11.9
T	0	1	0	0	0	0	0	0	1.8

	Parma	Hartsburgh	Milgrim	Martingale	Caddo	Delphi	Havencrest	Ipswich	St. Elmo	GAAS
40. If the faculty here think a bright kid is showing off they can be pretty clever at putting him in his place.										Key T
S	52†	59	56	70	66	70	64	60	86†	64.4
T	5	7	5	5	7	5	3	4	5	80.7
41. Students here know that poetry is supposed to be beautiful but deep down they also know that the biggest part of it is pure bunk. Key T										
S	47	42	62†	68†	42	41	45	14†	36	43.7
T	1	4	4	2	4	1	1	0	2	33.3
42. A student who gets on anybody's black list here has a pretty hard time; it practically takes a lawyer to get him off. Key T										
S	48	58	59*	45	41	46	42	52	57	49.2
T	3	3	1	4	3	0	2	3	2	36.9
43. Playing up to teachers and getting on their good side is the smart thing to do around here. Key T										
S	33*	53	56*	42	40	50	39	54	35	44.5
T	1	1	2	0	1	1	0	2	4	21.1
44. The administration tries to see to it that cliques don't get a chance to dominate in any activity. Key T										
S	37	36	49	43	41	59†	42	37	61†	44.8
T	6	5	2	3	3	6	4	2	4	61.5

45. You have to be concerned about marks here, that is, if you are going to get anywhere and be anything.   Key T

S	96	90	93	92	88	92	91	86	94	90.8
T	7	3	4	3	5	6	4	4	5	72.0

46. If a boy and a girl go steady here, the chances are that they are really in love.   Key F

S	85	81	80	73*	85	84	78	85	83	80.9
T	7	8	5	6	7	6	5	5	6	96.5

47. The students here like a teacher to be wrapped up in his subject even though he may demand a great deal from them.   Key F

S	43	45	49	46	54†	33	44	38	23†	41.0
T	1	0	0	2	2	1	1	0	0	12.3

48. Dances are heavily chaperoned here.   Key T

S	67†	51	56	35†	52	44	55	61*	40*	50.4
T	6	5	3	3	6	4	1	2	4	59.8

49. Students here know that it isn't easy to decide who was the best president the United States ever had.   Key F

S	11	13	12	16	14	5*	12	15	8	11.6
T	2	0	0	0	3	0	1	0	0	10.5

50. Initiations here are carefully controlled to see that there isn't any rough stuff.   Key T

S	71†	44†	66	62	65	48*	78†	27*	70*	58.2
T	5	3	2	4	4	3	6	2	5	59.8

	Parma	Hartsburgh	Milgrim	Martingale	Caddo	Delphi	Havencrest	Ipswich	St. Elmo	GAAS
51. Keeping everybody quiet when they're in the library is a regular cause with the librarians here. Key T										
S	87	73†	88	92*	82	84	71†	91*	79	82.7
T	4	5	5	6	6	5	3	4	6	77.1
52. If a teacher or administrator accuses a student of misbehavior here, there isn't much he can do to defend himself. Key T										
S	53	62	71*	55	60	58	50	66	64	59.4
T	1	3	0	1	2	1	2	2	2	24.6
53. To be an honor student here means that you really know a lot about the subjects you've taken. Key F										
S	41*	27	30	33	24	29	27	35	25	29.9
T	1	1	1	2	3	0	2	2	0	21.1
54. When you miss school for any reason, you have to have a note from your parents to get back in. Key T										
S	86†	45†	61	57	52	91†	9†	45†	100†	60.6
T	7	3	5	6	5	6	0	2	6	70.2
55. Teachers are too soft, too easy with the students here. They don't expect enough from them and don't make them work hard enough. Key T										
S	16	24*	26*	33†	18	8*	7†	17	3†	16.6
T	0	3	1	1	1	0	0	1	0	12.3

56. A basic principle of the way this school is supposed to be run is that everybody gets equal treatment no matter who he is. Key T

S	78	67*	70	73	77	76	77	86†	79	75.6
T	7	6	4	5	5	6	5	5	4	82.5

57. Students here found out in their English classes that Shakespeare wrote some really good plays. Key F

S	20	18	20	34†	9*	17	12	11	8*	16.5
T	2	0	0	0	0	0	0	0	0	3.5

58. We try not to have "stars" in sports here. The important thing is for everybody to get a chance to participate. Key T

S	32*	41	41	44	43	28†	43	64†	53*	42.8
T	6	4	3	3	2	5	6	6	1	53.1

59. Students here are serious about using their study time well. They just don't like it when somebody's fooling around and attracting attention, and they let him know it. Key F

S	89†	79*	73	84†	83†	65	66	54†	51†	71.1
T	6	8	5	6	5	3	2	4	3	73.6

60. If a freshman or sophomore seems to have a crush on one of the athletes around here, people either laugh at him or try to get him over it for his own good. Key T

S	25	30	30	32	24	36	31	17†	43†	29.5
T	0	0	0	0	0	1	1	1	4	12.3

	Parma	Hartsburgh	Milgrim	Martingale	Caddo	Delphi	Havencrest	Ipswich	St. Elmo	GAAS
61. It isn't how much you know, but it's how much you are willing to put up with that gets you good grades. Key T											
S	15†	34	39	61†	32	22*	34	26	25	31.9
T	0	0	1	0	1	0	0	1	1	7.0
62. Club and school activities here have to be planned and approved by the activities office a long way ahead of time. Key T											
S	77	79	77	70	80	83	82	70	80	77.1
T	5	5	2	1	7	6	3	1	3	58.0
63. Most students here are too proud to cheat on examinations. Key F											
S	73	81*	84†	85†	84†	63	66	43†	59*	70.3
T	4	4	4	5	5	3	2	2	1	52.6
64. The administration has succeeded in getting "hell week" replaced by "help week"; pledges go out and help in hospitals and such places instead of being hazed. Key T											
S	41	23*	35	20†	24	31	45†	27	51†	32.4
T	3	0	3	0	1	2	2	2	4	29.8
65. Our guidance people are really helpful when it comes to advice about careers and college. Key F											
S	12	18	11	18	15	16	13	56†	4†	18.0
T	0	0	0	0	0	1	0	1	0	3.5

66. Any student whose grades aren't as good as his IQ shows they ought to be is likely to be called in and counseled as an "underachiever." Key T

S	43	55	52	43	51	39	27†	33†	82†	46.8
T	6	4	6	4	6	4	4	3	6	75.0

67. There are teachers here who when they tell you your work is well done you know it is good. Key F

S	2	5	6	9	3	3	1	7	4	4.4
T	0	0	0	0	0	0	0	0	0	0.0

68. When you miss school on account of illness, you have to bring a note from your doctor. Key T

S	17	20	19	30*	8†	10†	25	34†	27	21.1
T	2	3	0	1	0	0	4	0	3	22.8

69. Some teachers here make you feel like you don't know anything. Key T

S	65	71	76*	69	61	78†	67	56	46†	65.2
T	3	5	4	6	3	4	3	5		66.8

70. Our guidance people are on the lookout for problems; they don't wait for the student to indicate he *wants* help. Key T

S	61	51	54	69†	54	46	42*	31†	65†	52.0
T	7	5	2	6	7	5	4	3	5	77.1

71. There are students here who could gain a great deal from a good art appreciation course. Key F

S	20	20	12	15	17	12	18	20	23	17.3
T	0	0	0	0	0	0	0	0	0	0.0

	Parma	Hartsburgh	Milgrim	Martingale	Caddo	Delphi	Havencrest	Ipswich	St. Elmo	GAAS
72. Anybody who is really good at anything is looked up to around here, whether it is jazz, playing ball, or classwork. Key F										
S	21	23	28	31	23	22	26	26	32	25.6
T	0	1	2	2	1	1	2	0	0	15.8
73. The school puts students it thinks are dumb in separate classes from the rest. Key T										
S	48	32†	64†	69†	66†	50	55	19†	56	50.4
T	6	8	5	6	7	6	3	3	5	86.0
74. When a boy and a girl fall in love around here, other people usually respect their feelings and leave them alone. Key F										
S	30	22*	28	50†	29	30	22*	36	45†	32.2
T	5	2	3	2	2	1	2	1	4	38.6
75. Many of the teachers know a great deal about things other than what they cover in their subject in class. Key F										
S	3	10	2	9	6	0	5	7	1	4.7
T	0	1	0	1	0	0	0	0	0	3.5

PHASE I TESTING

PART II: A SUPPLEMENTARY ANALYSIS OF THE SCHOOLS

ALL of the nine secondary schools participating in this study are located along the Atlantic Coast. Five of the public schools, namely, Parma, Hartsburgh, Milgrim, Martingale, and Caddo, are in or near the same major metropolitan area. One of the independent schools, Ipswich, is also in the vicinity of this metropolis, and the other, St. Elmo, is situated in the core city itself. Delphi is adjacent to another major Eastern metropolis, and Havencrest, while at a considerable distance from the other schools, is also on the Coast. It is not, however, near a metropolitan area, as are the other schools.

Except for St. Elmo, which is a boys' school, all the participating schools are coeducational. Parma, Hartsburgh, Milgrim, Martingale, and Caddo are all within the same state. Delphi and Havencrest are in different states altogether. The two independent schools, Ipswich and St. Elmo, both operate under a religious aegis, Ipswich being nominally Protestant in its orientation and St. Elmo Catholic.

The nine schools serve students from families of very different social and economic statuses. A comparison in terms of the median and range of family incomes is reported in Table 1. As the basic data for this table is derived from Census Tracts, comparisons can only be made for the seven public schools.

With two exceptions, the relative ranking of the seven public

Table 1. Relative Family Income for Census Districts
Containing the Public Schools

School	Poverty-Deprivation ($0-4,999)	Adequate ($5,000-8,999)	Affluent ($9,000 & over)	Median Family Income
Delphi	8.2%	21.7%	70.1%	$10,000 +
Parma	15.6	46.5	37.9	7,977
Hartsburgh	24.7	45.8	29.5	6,894
Havencrest	30.9	42.4	26.7	6,465*
Milgrim	22.6	59.9	17.5	6,458
Martingale	35.2	54.5	10.3	5,854
Caddo	36.0	49.9	14.1	5,830

* The Negro population of Havencrest approximately 20%, is excluded
from these data because the school is not integrated.

Source: U.S. Census (1960). All data contained in this table refer to
census districts containing major sections of the school districts reported on in this project. It should be noted, however, that since boun-
daries of census and school districts almost never coincide, these figures
must be considered only approximate.

schools represented in Table 1 is confirmed by other census data.[1]
The exceptions are Havencrest and Martingale. Generally, Havencrest rates a little higher than this table indicates, approximating
Parma, because in Havencrest both prices and incomes are lower
compared with the rest of the country than in the other areas studied; therefore, money has more value there. Havencrest families
also have higher status positions than their incomes alone would
indicate. Martingale, on the other hand, sinks, relatively speaking,
and especially so when a skill rating for occupations is used. It then
falls considerably below Caddo. Only 5.7 percent of Martingale's
fathers are in professional, technical, and management positions
while at Caddo the figure stands at 16.2 percent, and at Delphi,
57.7 percent. Conversely, 53.7 percent of Martingale's fathers
are classified as unskilled workers—that is, as laborers, service

[1] The tables from which this generalization is drawn can be found in
The Project Report, CRP 1758, Appendix C, esp. pages 152-154.

workers, household workers, and operatives—as against 34.3 percent for Caddo and 8.6 percent for Delphi. Such figures undoubtedly reflect a pattern of job discriminatory practices at Martingale, a locality where 59.2 percent of the population is classified according to the 1960 U. S. Census as Negro.

Census data also reveal that Martingale apparently has a severe and continuing dropout problem. Whereas high school enrollment as a percentage of the fourteen- to seventeen-year-old population of the several districts conventionally ranges around 89 percent, with Milgrim at a low of 83.7 percent and Hartsburgh high for the seven schools with 94.2 percent, Martingale reports only 64.5 percent of its young people of these ages in school. These and other comparisons, then, suggest that Martingale should be ranked lowest according to socioeconomic criteria.

To summarize these data, a reasonable socioeconomic positioning of the participating public schools would place Delphi at the top, followed in order of descent by Parma, Havencrest, Hartsburgh, Milgrim, Caddo, and Martingale. Of these, Havencrest ranks somewhat higher than income figures alone would indicate and Martingale considerably lower.

There are, unfortunately, no comparable data for Ipswich or St. Elmo. Using reported fathers' occupations and the observations of project team members as our basis, we estimate that Ipswich rates about equal to or somewhat above Delphi in socioeconomic status. The situation at St. Elmo, with its core city location, is even more complex, and any such rating for that school is of dubious value. Some of the young men attending there are quite wealthy while others come from families that verge on poverty. In several cases great sacrifices had been made so that a son could attend St. Elmo.

On contacting each school, Professor Gold requested that a sample of the student body, consisting of approximately 100 students and 6 teachers, be invited to participate in the project. The students were to be chosen by the nth-name random technique; the teachers, wherever possible, were to be persons responsible for policy-making in the school. In all, 902 students subjects were tested during Phase I. Of these, 247 were included in Phase II testing. While the median school year of the sample group was the junior year (eleventh grade), there were sixty-four more sophomores than seniors in Phase I testing. This bias in favor of sophomores is also carried through to Phase II, where twenty more sophomores took the tests than did seniors. Nineteen ninth-graders were included in the Phase I sample, sixteen from Ipswich alone. The student subjects averaged sixteen years of age for both phases of the testing. Table 2 singles out certain other relevant characteristics of the sample. The schools are listed in the order of their ressentiment scores.

Table 2. Data on Subjects Participating in Phase I Testing

| School | Respondents | | | Program | | | Mean Grade Av. | Teacher Subjects |
	M	F	Total	Academic	Other	Unknown		
Martingale	49	55	104	65	36	3	77.3	6
Milgrim	48	46	94	51	39	4	76.7	5
Parma	48	52	100	85	15	0	81.5	7
Hartsburgh	49	48	97	73	21	3	78.9	8
Caddo	42	52	94	58	36	0	78.5	7
St. Elmo	100	0	100	99	1	0	84.1	6
Delphi	59	53	112	92	15	5	81.5	6
Havencrest	48	52	100	96	4	0	80.3	6
Ipswich	53	48	101	93	2	6	80.2	6
All Schools	496	406	902	712	169	21		57

As might be expected, socioeconomic conditions are reflected in the programs in which the students are enrolled. At Delphi and Parma the young people are overwhelmingly academic whereas at Caddo and Martingale a large proportion of the student body registers as commercial or general. Havencrest and Milgrim are exceptions. The first is an exception for reasons associated with state policy; the second, Milgrim, is so for less obvious reasons. Here, despite its middle-range social positioning, relatively few students are registered in the academic program.

The comparison of the Mean Grade Averages[2] recorded in Table 2 is even more interesting, for socioeconomic positioning is again reflected. Milgrim once more is an anomaly. Its students report the lowest grade average of any school. Here, the two independent schools can be brought into the comparison: St. Elmo reports the highest grade achievement of any school; Ipswich is somewhat low, considering its high status rating.

Professor Gold's evaluative report describes these schools as a unit in terms of educational procedures. He begins his report, "In spite of the reasonably diverse socioeconomic and geographical backgrounds of the pupil populations at the various schools, all reflect what is essentially a kindred secondary school curriculum supported by a consanguinity of instructional methodology.

"Furthermore," he continues, "observations of classrooms in session revealed that the prime method of instruction at all schools consisted of lectures fused with teacher-directed question-and-answer periods. Only at Ipswich and Havencrest were opportunities for group discussion in evidence to any degree. In a similar vein most of the classes that were observed could be typified as 'orderly' and essentially 'textbook-centered.' Here again, Havencrest, Ipswich, and to a lesser extent Delphi, tempered their curriculum by attempting to individualize instruction in terms of student interests and needs. Most of the classrooms observed were centered squarely on the teacher in charge. That is to say, they were conducted in a manner similar to that manifested by the leader of a symphony orchestra, with permission to participate allotted to specific individuals at specific times. Rarely were students given the chance to discuss the subject being studied with each other. In some instances where the instructor tried to stimulate discussion, the awkwardness of the result suggested that this was a special technique 'put on' for the benefit of the observer. Comfortable interpersonal relationships were, however, occasionally observed at both Milgrim and Caddo, in addition to the previously cited Ipswich and Havencrest. At the other extreme, participation of an interactive nature was never observed at either Parma or St. Elmo.

[2] Letter grades and numerical grades are reconciled according to the following scheme: D = 65, D+ = 68, C− = 72, C = 75, C+ = 78, B− = 82, B = 85, B+ = 88, A− = 92, A = 95.

"Similarly," Gold continues, "observed teacher control devices ranged from motivating interest in the dignity of the subject matter, most prevalent at Havencrest and Ipswich, to scolding and threatening students, most evident at Martingale and Caddo. The converse of the latter technique—praise and rewards—was again most in evidence at Martingale, and to a lesser extent at St. Elmo. Interest in classroom activities was also rated in each of the schools. It appeared to be highest at Delphi and St. Elmo and lowest at Milgrim, where more students gave the impression of being uninterested than interested in their work."

In his discussion of responses to the Non-Verbal Perception Test, in which respondents were asked to draw an ideal social studies classroom, Gold reports, "Responses again are particularly revealing with reference to the uniformity of the various schools studied. Intended as an instrument that would enable students to reflect divergent as well as convergent thinking processes, it revealed only the latter. There were rarely any divergent responses, no matter what school was being studied. Although students embellished their designs with an occasional ash tray or bathroom, responses were overwhelmingly convergent. The test, however, did give students an opportunity to articulate certain impressions of their schools. For example, the boys at St. Elmo included more podia and platforms for the teachers, the students at Delphi and Havencrest drew more semiformal seminar classroom structures, and Ipswich students depicted classrooms that were the most informal of all. At Caddo and Martingale, on the other hand, the classrooms were, as a totality, composed of neatly arranged rows of desks facing the chalkboard. And at Milgrim more bathrooms were included in the classroom designs there—reflecting the oppressive restrictions regarding physical movement at that school."

In sum, then, Gold's project evaluation report testified to the existence of an omnipresent and inexorable compulsion shaping events in the schools, instituting a depressing sameness everywhere. School-by-school variation was found to be minor, with such distinctions that existed emerging in shades of gray, not in stark contradictions of black and white.

In contrast to this flatness was the enthusiasm generated in response to the Best Thing-Worst Thing Test. In this test students were asked to describe events having meaning for them. They embraced these instructions with spirit. Meaning was important to them. Witness, for instance, this short Best Thing by Charley Johnson of Milgrim, "The day I asked this girl to go with me. I felt like a king." And even the Worst Things have their poignancy, combined generally with a touch of asperity. Pat Smith of Parma, in another short statement, offered this as her Worst Thing, "I moved here . . . and met the kids."

Such comments may sometimes not be nice, but they certainly projected authenticity. In the course of our discussion of the individual schools we made extensive use of responses to the Best Thing-Worst Thing Test, because they, more than any other instrument, amplified the temper peculiar to each of the schools. In this way, along with the Non-Verbal Perception Test, these responses served as useful supplements to the instrument designed to measure the intensity of ressentiment in the schools.

This instrument, the F-N R Index combined with the Stern Index items, allowed a maximum possible R score of 135. Were such a score reported it would have indicated that the subject so reporting had agreed with the prescribed key in his response to each and every one of the statements comprising the combined indexes. The minimum score possible was zero. The true mean score for the 880 subjects who completed the test was 62.4, with the highest R score recorded as 99 and the lowest 30. (See Table 3 in text, p. 107.)

Clearly, the subject schools break into three relatively distinct groups, with Martingale and Milgrim at the top, with Parma, Hartsburgh, Caddo, and St. Elmo in a group clustered around the average for all nine schools, and with Delphi, Havencrest, and Ipswich at the bottom. When tested with a standard T-test for significance, the groups hold up. The means recorded for Martingale and Milgrim do not differ significantly from each other at the 1 percent level but they do from Hartsburgh, the next highest school. These same stipulations hold for the group of four central schools—Parma, Hartsburgh, Caddo, and St. Elmo—and for the three bottom schools—Delphi, Havencrest, and Ipswich—although the difference in means between the boundary schools, St. Elmo and Delphi, is not as strong. There the difference is significant at the 2 percent level but not at the 1 percent level.

Again, the socioeconomic positioning repeats itself, with variations similar to those adduced earlier. In terms of rated ressentiment the public schools descend from Martingale: Milgrim, Hartsburgh, Parma, Caddo, Delphi, Havencrest; and in status terms rather than incomes they ascend to Martingale: Caddo, Milgrim, Hartsburgh, Havencrest, Parma, Delphi. Out of place are Caddo and Havencrest. The anomaly of Milgrim also continues: it only just misses obtaining the highest score of all in ressentiment. Of the independent schools, Ipswich scores lowest of all schools, and St. Elmo ranks a little higher than might have been expected.

Clearly, proposition (2), in which we postulated that ressentiment would be most intense in lower class schools with middle class teachers and least intense in public and private schools with an upper class orientation, is supported by these findings. At the same time, however, when we compare responses from the R index with those from the Q-sort testing, we find that the two lower class schools, Martingale and Milgrim, along with Ipswich, produce the largest number of putative adolescents. It would seem, then, that while ressentiment is intense in those two schools, it is not as effective in encouraging conventionalism as in several of the more middle class schools.

Appendix B

PHASE II TESTING:
THE Q-SORT EPISODES

[PHASE II testing, which sought to assess the impact of different school environments on students, consisted of six serially related Q-sort instruments. The first episode presented to our subjects, which is also the simplest, is called *The Clarke-Barto Incident*. The narrative to which our subjects were requested to relate their card choices was, in this case, deliberately kept simple so that the subject could become familiar with the comparatively complex procedure before having to deal with complexities in the episode itself. *The Clarke-Barto Incident* was also the first episode written for the study; it was completed even before we had decided to give our imaginary high school a name—LeMoyen High School.]

Episode I—The Clarke-Barto Incident [1]

Suppose that your school is strict in enforcing the rule against students smoking in washrooms. The following incident takes place:

Mr. Arthur Clarke, a social studies teacher at your school, is taking his mid-morning coffee-break. On entering a men's wash-

[1] The episodes and the student tables in this appendix also appear in *Coming of Age in America,* by Edgar Z. Friedenberg. © Copyright 1965 by Edgar Z. Friedenberg. Reprinted by permission of Random House, Inc.

room he discovers Johnny Barto, a junior and a somewhat notorious character around the school, smoking. Mr. Clarke knows that Johnny should be in class at this hour and furthermore that he is a troublemaker, is having difficulty with his courses, is on probation, and that he is old enough to quit school. While Mr. Clarke and Johnny are approximately the same size, Johnny is not very strong. His whole attitude, though, is one of arrogance, as if to say, "Show me, buddy."

Now turn to the cards you have been given. On these cards you will find stated nine possible actions which Mr. Clarke might have taken on discovering Johnny. While it is also true that he might have undertaken to perform a combination of several of these, or might also have done something entirely different, disregard this. *For the moment,* think only in terms of each of these as separate and alternative actions. You will have sufficient opportunity after completing the test to discuss the adequacy of these separate actions. Please read *all the cards* through thoroughly. Then, having read them through:

(1) Select the three cards which, you feel, represent the best actions that could have been taken under the circumstances.

(2) From these three, select the one action which you think would have been best of all.

(3) Returning to the cards remaining, select the three cards which you feel represent the worst actions that could have been taken under the circumstances.

(4) From these three, select the one action which you feel would be worst of all.

You should now have the cards arranged symmetrically in piles of 1, 2, 3, 2, 1 along an axis indicating the way you favor them as reactions to the situation described.

[These directions, with minor variations in wording to fit the situation described in the narrative episode, are standard for all six episodes and will not be repeated in detail again.

For the actual testing, the comments, which are listed below, were printed on separate cards with no identifying numbers. The comments were numbered to enable us to keep track of them during the analysis. Immediately following the comments for the episode, and for each of the subsequent episodes, we have included in tabular form the results of the testing. The reader might find it interesting and instructive to compare his personal choices with those of our respondents.]

1. Mr. Clarke orders Johnny to put the cigarette out and return to class. Johnny responds by taking a swing at Clarke. Clarke, angry himself now, knocks Johnny down. Afterwards, he helps Johnny to his feet and apologizes for his anger but warns Johnny he will report him if he catches him smoking illegally again.

2. To teach Johnny a lesson Mr. Clarke strikes him several times. This he does coolly and with emotional restraint. After finishing, he gives Johnny a lecture, telling him what happens to young men like him when they don't mend their ways.

3. Mr. Clarke orders Johnny to report to his (Clarke's) classroom the next period. At that time Clarke describes the incident to the class, and then orders Johnny to apologize to the students for having brought the good name of the school into disrepute. After the apology, Mr. Clarke asks the class members to suggest appropriate punishment for Johnny. This is all presented as a kind of object lesson in social studies.

4. Mr. Clarke takes Johnny to the principal's office and turns him over to the person on duty there for punishment. He also requests of the office that it notify him as to the nature and severity of the punishment to be administered to Johnny.

5. Mr. Clarke reports Johnny to the Student Court at their meeting that evening. At the time he calls on the officers of the Court to remember their responsibility for the maintenance of order in the school, warns them not to be swayed by sentiment, and then requests that suitable punishment be administered.

6. Mr. Clarke calls Johnny's parents, describes the incident to them, informs them of the seriousness of the offense, and suggests that they take appropriate measures to get Johnny in line. He also warns them that if they do not succeed, it will reflect against Johnny.

7. Mr. Clarke has Johnny report for after-school detention, at which time he (Clarke) has Johnny write the following statement on the blackboard 500 times, "I, Johnny Barto, am sorry and will never smoke in school again."

8. At the faculty meeting that afternoon, Mr. Clarke discusses

the "Johnny Barto problem" with the school psychologist, and the school psychologist agrees to set up a counseling program designed to get at Johnny's "antisocial" behavior and straighten him out. The psychologist then calls Johnny in for counseling.

9. Mr. Clarke acts as if he hadn't noticed Johnny and leaves the washroom as soon as possible.

[Our subjects' card choices for *The Clarke-Barto Incident* are summarized in Table 1. The cards are listed in descending order of popularity, according to their Grand Average Pile Placement (GAPP). To compute the GAPP take, for example, Card (1) for the episode. For this card 4 respondents chose it as their Best choice, 33 as a Good choice, 110 were neutral about the card, 90 looked on it as Poor, and 10 thought it Worst of the lot. To compute an average a 9-point scale was used, with Best rating as +4, Good as +2.5, neutral as 0, Poor as −2.5, and Worst as −4. On this scale the GAPP (average placement for all respondents) is −.67 (rounded off to −.7 in Table 1). GAPP's have been computed for each of the nine cards of the six episodes (54 in all) and are recorded in the tables.]

Table 1. Students' Card Choices for *The Clarke-Barto Incident*

Card Pile Placement	Best	Good	Neutral	Poor	Worst	GAPP
(8) School psychologist	116	75	48	7	1	2.6
(6) Calls parents	54	127	62	3	1	2.1
(4) Sends to principal	38	110	82	17	0	1.6
(5) Student Court	25	112	96	11	3	1.4
(1) Johnny fights Clarke	4	33	110	90	10	− 0.7
(7) Writes on blackboard	2	10	147	81	7	− 0.8
(3) A class example	5	14	104	83	41	− 1.3
(2) Clarke beats Johnny	1	4	49	115	78	− 2.4
(9) Clarke does nothing	2	9	43	87	106	− 2.5
Sum (N = 247)	247	494	741	494	247	

Episode II—The LeMoyen Basketball Team

At LeMoyen High School, about a fifth of the students are Negro; the rest include young people of Irish, Italian, and Eastern European descent—the last, chiefly of the Jewish faith—as well as some students from families that migrated from Northern Europe several generations back and think of themselves as just Americans. Because of the way the neighborhood served by LeMoyen High School has developed, the Negro students come from homes in which the father, on the average, earns more money and has had more years of education than the fathers of the average white students at LeMoyen, who are mostly from working class families.

For the past two years LeMoyen has had the best basketball team anywhere around and has won the regional championship. The seventeen-man squad has ten Negroes on it and five boys from Irish families. Three of the four regular starters on the highly successful team are Negro players, while the fourth is a white student named Johnny Adams. The coach, Mr. Regan, who also teaches shop, passes the fifth starting position around among the Irish lads on his bench. There has never been a Jewish boy on the basketball team at LeMoyen. Mr. Regan says the Jewish boys are "fine students, but too short to make good ball players."

This year, there transferred into LeMoyen, as a Junior, a boy from an Irish background whose father was recently sent to the community as director of plant operations for the oil refinery that is by far the biggest industry in town. The only LeMoyen student this boy, Kevin McGuire, knew before he came to town was Grant Eubanks, the captain of the basketball team and the son of a Negro physician who is the chief heart specialist at the local Veterans' Hospital. The two met at a camp in France where students from other countries go to spend the summer and work with French people and get to know them. McGuire, who as a sophomore was already a basketball star at his old high school, was drawn to Eubanks by the game; during the summer they taught about fifty kids of various nationalities, who had never seen a game, to play fairly good basketball. Eubanks told Mr. Regan that the six-foot-five McGuire is without a doubt the best basketball player ever to come anywhere near LeMoyen and that they must get him on the team. At this moment, McGuire is driving over to the gym to try out for the team, and Mr. Regan is trying to decide what to do next.

1. The only important thing for Mr. Regan to consider is whether McGuire is as good a player as Eubanks thinks he is. This is what should determine whether a boy gets on the team; the rest of the story is irrelevant.

2. If he doesn't want things to get out of hand, Mr. Regan had better take a hard look now at what basketball is being used for at LeMoyen. The business of a high school basketball coach isn't to win games but to give every boy his fair chance to participate, even if he isn't such an expert.

3. If Mr. Regan is the kind of coach who puts competence above race or religion, he and the LeMoyen team will surely welcome young McGuire with unmixed delight.

4. There doesn't seem to be too much of a moral issue here, but, politically, Mr. Regan is certainly on the spot.

5. Mr. Regan might find it very helpful if it were pointed out to him that letting young McGuire join the team would not really be in the best interests of either the boy or the school. Having the richest boy in school as a star athlete as well would be very likely to lead the basketball team to think of itself as a group of privileged characters—which, under the particular circumstances described, would be most unfortunate.

6. Mr. Regan is being offered another top-flight player who comes sponsored by his captain and has the same national background as the boys on the team who haven't been doing so well. McGuire sounds like just what he needs.

7. A basketball team is an official school organization, and official school organizations should be representative. It is the responsibility of the principal and the Board to see to it that the basketball coach—no matter who he is—runs the team for the benefit of the whole school and not as his private club.

8. It is too risky to take McGuire on the team, especially if he is as good as Eubanks says he is. Coming from a rich home, and as Eubanks' friend, it would be the last straw for the poor Irish boys. You can't really expect them to take a thing like that. A team may like to have stars, but it needs its back bench, too.

9. This story shows how two boys who share the same skill and enthusiasm in sports and general social background can accept each other as individuals, without getting involved in an irrelevant racial issue. Their problem now is just to finish what they have started; Mr. Regan will be risking upsetting his team by letting Mc-Guire on it; but if he is really a good teacher and a good man he must do it.

Table 2. Students' Card Choices for *The LeMoyen Basketball Team*

Card Pile Placement	Best	Good	Neutral	Poor	Worst	GAPP
(3) Unmixed delight	53	128	51	11	4	2.0
(1) Only important thing	91	69	35	36	16	1.6
(7) Official school organization	34	81	100	25	7	1.0
(9) Irrelevant racial issue	27	69	115	31	5	0.7
(2) Isn't to win games	22	53	115	49	8	0.3
(6) Just what he needs	15	67	104	40	21	0.2
(4) No moral issue	1	7	128	71	40	− 1.3
(5) Might find it very helpful	2	12	48	115	70	− 2.1
(8) Too risky	2	8	45	116	76	− 2.3
Sum (N = 247)	247	494	741	494	247	

Episode III—The LeMoyen Dance

The Student Council at LeMoyen High School is planning the annual Spring Dance. This event is held in the high school auditorium, and about one forth of the cost of it is covered by a subsidy from the school. The rest of the money must be raised by selling "bids" (or admission tickets) and refreshments. The dance has been held every year for the past six years and has become more and more popular each year. It is open to any LeMoyen student. Bids are generally $1.50 per couple or $1 stag. Refreshments have consisted of hot dogs, hamburgers, and pizza slices at 35¢ each and soft drinks at a quarter. The music for the dance is recorded. Last year, a large proportion of the junior and senior classes attended the dance—over three hundred couples and about seventy-five stags. Except for an occasional girl dated by an older boy, freshmen and sophomores rarely attend.

However, last year's dance was marred by the obstreperous behavior of several stags who appeared to have drunk their fill, and whom the teachers who were designated to act as chaperones were unable to keep at bay. Afterwards, a rumor went around the school that these boys had been "troublemakers" from the school's vocational track, though vocational students have generally supported the Spring Dance enthusiastically. "They get *so* much out of it," Miss Leigh, the speech and drama teacher who has served as chaperone since the first dance was held, had earlier observed. "It's the one big event of the year for them." And, in fact, the only students who were actually identified as contributing to the disorder that broke out on the floor were seniors, now in college, who, the Dean of Boys reported sadly to Miss Leigh afterwards, "come from some of the finest homes in the city—I never thought I would have to call them into the office." "I'm sorry, sir," one of these boys told the dean. "We didn't particularly want to spoil anybody's good time, but the whole thing was so jammed you couldn't move, and it has gotten so *corny* it didn't even seem real. I mean, like, we go to dances all the time, and, *you* know."

Though the dean accepted this explanation and let the boys off with a reprimand, pointing out to them that their conduct had shown them to be deficient in just the qualities of leadership he had counted on them to have, the Student Council is anxious to avoid any repetition of the disaster this year. Accordingly, one faction of the students on the Council has proposed a radical revision of the plans. These suggest that the price of the bids be raised to $7.50, a couple or stag, and that the cost of the refreshments be included. For this money, they calculated that they could provide a tempting cold buffet, or *smörgåsbord,* and that they could also hire a small orchestra that the school jazz club has said is the coolest in town. Although the Student Council has final responsibility for planning the dance, it has held a survey of school opinion to guide it in reaching a decision. The survey indicates:

(1) A majority of the entire student body oppose the new, more expensive plan.

(2) A small majority of the students who attended last year's dance, however, favor the new plan.

(3) Enough students indicated that they would still attend if the price of bids was raised to $7.50, with supper included, to give a predicted attendance of about a hundred couples. This is enough, by a wide margin, to pay for the dance.

1. It is hard to see how the Student Council can persist with such an undemocratic plan, when their own study shows that a majority of the student body oppose it. It is their duty as elected representatives to find another, more acceptable solution.

2. It is unfortunate that the Student Council should be obliged to consider making the Spring Dance a more exclusive affair, but they may have to do it. Evidently, as the dance has gotten more and more popular, it has attracted the kind of "teen-ager" who does not know how to act at a dance. The somewhat greater formality and higher cost of attending the dance under the new proposal should limit its appeal to the kind of student who belongs there.

3. A serious disadvantage of the new plan is that some youngsters would be excluded from the Spring Dance who would enjoy it, simply because they couldn't afford it anymore. But this may be outweighed by the fact that it would be a much better dance, even if you had to save up or go without something else. If the dance is allowed to turn into a brawl or a ratrace, it isn't worth holding.

4. There is nothing undemocratic about the Student Council's new plan. A majority of the students who are qualified to pass judgment, and who have shown their interest by supporting the dance last year, approve the new plan. And it would still be open to any student who wanted to spend the money.

5. The Student Council has been left holding the bag for the Dean of Boys' reluctance to treat kids from influential families like everybody else. If he had cracked down on these boys after last year's dance, there wouldn't be any problem.

6. Everything the school sponsors is a part of its educational

program and should be open to all. It is good for the Student Council to have the experience of running the dance, as this helps them to learn to be responsible. But they must not be permitted to turn public education into an exclusive social affair.

7. Maybe the dance is pretty corny and crowded. But it wouldn't be fair to turn it into a college-type affair that most of the students would not feel at home at, especially those who have not had the advantages of the youngsters from better homes. Chaperone the dance a little more closely, if necessary, but keep it down to earth and unpretentious, the way it is now.

8. Unfortunately, the Student Council is not the proper body to get to the root of a problem like this. Youngsters have to learn—sometimes the hard way—to bear the responsibility for their own misconduct. The school authorities should suspend the dance for a year, to teach the students that the privilege of holding it depends on their power to discipline their own conduct. This is a far more important question than what kind of a dance they have.

9. If you are planning a dance, the first consideration is to make it a good one. Dances don't break up into brawls unless the kids are pretty bored with them. The new plan would make this a really

Table 3. Students' Card Choices for *The LeMoyen Dance*

Card Pile Placement	Best	Good	Neutral	Poor	Worst	GAPP
(7) Keep unpretentious	45	69	91	40	1	1.0
(3) Brawl or ratrace	39	75	87	33	12	0.9
(1) More acceptable solution	47	63	82	45	9	0.8
(6) Exclusive social affair	29	67	99	43	8	0.6
(9) Can get awfully tired	37	57	97	43	12	0.6
(5) Cracked down	11	44	105	68	18	− 0.4
(4) There is nothing	11	60	70	71	34	− 0.5
(2) It is unfortunate	21	41	64	79	41	− 0.7
(8) Suspend the dance	6	16	43	70	111	− 2.3
Sum (N = 246)	246	492	738	492	246	

enjoyable occasion and might especially benefit the less privileged kids, who can get awfully tired, too, of cheap, commonplace, institutionalized entertainment.

Table 4. Teachers' Card Choices for *The LeMoyen Dance*

Card Pile Placement	Best	Good	Neutral	Poor	Worst	GAPP
(6) Exclusive social affair	18	19	13	3	2	1.9
(7) Keep unpretentious	8	26	13	7	1	1.3
(1) More acceptable solution	12	18	17	7	1	1.3
(3) Brawl or ratrace	5	16	28	4	2	0.8
(9) Can get awfully tired	4	11	26	9	5	0.0
(5) Cracked down	3	7	18	17	10	−1.0
(4) There is nothing	0	4	22	22	7	−1.3
(8) Suspend the dance	3	7	12	16	17	−1.4
(2) It is unfortunate	2	2	16	25	10	−1.6
Sum (N = 55)	55	110	165	110	55	

Episode IV—The King's Visit

Several weeks ago, the Governor wrote the principal of LeMoyen High School to tell him about the impending visit to Capital City of the King of a country not unlike Denmark and of the King's notable interest in spirited young people. He also informed the principal of the King's expressed desire to meet with some interesting and representative high school students during his visit. The Governor then went on to say that he had selected LeMoyen as one of the ten high schools from throughout the state which were to pick several students to meet with the King when he visits the Governor at the executive mansion. The Governor added that the King speaks English fluently and then concluded with the suggestion that such young people as were to be chosen should be persons to whom the school could point with pride as expressing what was finest and best about their school.

At LeMoyen, where such things are always done as democratically as possible, the students were to have a voice in the choice. First, nine individuals and groups were nominated by a committee composed jointly of faculty members and students, with the Dean of Men, Mr. Blakely, serving as chairman. These nine were to stand for election as candidates for the post of school representative (or representatives). The student body was to choose from this list of nine the person or persons they thought would best represent them at the meeting with the King. This vote was not conclusive, however, but was primarily advisory, for the principal reserved the right to make the final nomination for the school, guiding himself in his choice by the committee recommendations and the student vote.

The committee has just acted and the nine candidates have been chosen. They include:

1. Nancy Harris.

Nancy Harris is a violinist. This year she has been accorded the signal honor of being first violinist and concert master of the all-state orchestra. She has also performed as soloist for several of the local symphony orchestras. Nancy is gifted with artistic sensibility and quickness in all things. She is a very good student and still manages to keep her coursework up while practicing three or four hours a day. Unfortunately, her schedule does not allow her much opportunity for social activity, which is too bad because she is really an attractive young lady who, with a little effort, could easily be very popular. But her enthusiasms are more for things than for people and she prefers artistic creation to success with her fellow students.

2. Eric Pratt.

Everybody at LeMoyen loves Eric Pratt. He's cool. He has a great line and really knows how to make the girls happy. He's always lots of fun, anywhere, any time. He's up on the latest record, in with the newest fad, and on to the easiest way to do the hard things. Eric's sharp, he sure is; you should see the way he dresses. Man, you should see. If you had money like Eric has you could pay for the clothes, but I'll bet you couldn't get it right, most likely you wouldn't. It's something you've got to know how to do, and Eric does. He's got style in everything he does. Don't get the idea that this kid's just popular with the gang, though. He's more than that. The teachers think he's great, too, especially the women teachers. He knows how to talk to them, and make them love him, and make them do anything he wants them to do.

3. Elfrieda Eubanks.

Elfrieda Eubanks is so sweet you couldn't help liking her, and everybody at LeMoyen does. She's president of the Girls' Athletic Association and a sure thing for the Chamber of Commerce's Best All-Around Girl award this spring. Elfrieda is tall, slender, and very graceful. She has a beautiful voice and sings regularly at several local churches. A better-than-average student, she's also a volunteer nurse's aide at the hospital, chairman of the school hostess club, and LeMoyen's number-one cheerleader. She dances beautifully, too. One thing you can say about Elfrieda—she's always smiling, always a good guy, no matter what. That's what makes her so popular. Even her twin brother, Grant, who was the best basketball player LeMoyen had until Kevin McGuire came along, isn't as popular as Elfrieda, and that's saying something.

4. Johnny Adams.

Johnny Adams is something of an enigma. It isn't easy to figure out how he managed to make the basketball team. He's not big and he's not fast. It's not clear why he wanted to, either. He doesn't hang around with the fellows on the team. The kids he runs around with are what are called beatniks at LeMoyen, the kind, you know, who usually don't care about things like sports and dances. But when Johnny decided he wanted to make the team, he did. He has drive, and he's smart, too. If he wanted to, he's one fellow who could give Karen Clarke or Scott Cowen a real run for it academically. But most of the time he doesn't feel like it. When he does, though, watch out. It was a big surprise last year when he won the Veterans' Club oratorical contest. He did it against odds, too. No one would ever call him good-looking; he has a sort of squeaky voice, and most of the time he could use a haircut and shave. He's not always an easy guy to be with, either. Still, he took on the best the county had to offer and showed them all how to do it.

5. Ronnie, Big Joe, and Pink.

Ronnie, Big Joe, and Pink have just cut their second platter. Known as the Combo, they play and sing with a fast, easy beat that's sometimes subtle and sometimes frantic. It's easy to like, too. The Combo is so good, actually, that it was featured on a coast-to-coast TV network last month. About the members of the Combo, well, they're not just ordinary: Big Joe, Joe White, that is, is the first Negro ever to be elected president of the school honor society. Pincus Peabody is going to a music school in New York on a scholarship next year. He's quite a composer and works up the arrangements for the Combo. He can write in the classical mood also and is the composer of the violin sonatina Nancy Harris is planning to play at graduation. One can't say too much for Ronnie, though, except that he organized the Combo and writes the lyrics. And really, the lyrics are great, they have a twist to them that gives them class, something like the Kingston Trio, and still it's different.

6. Karen Clarke.

Karen Clarke will be giving the valedictory at graduation for this year's class. As she should. Always well-groomed and polite, she is completely in command of herself in any situation. She is the perfect model of what a high school student ought to be. Her work is neat, correct, and, unlike so many other students', in on time. It really has to be because her dad, Mr. Clarke, teaches here and he makes sure Karen doesn't get any special favors. He makes certain that she stands up for herself and does her work. In student activities she is treasurer of the senior class. She is also a teacher's aide for Mr. Pottitione's chemistry laboratory and a member of the Ethics Committee of the Student Government. Where others are concerned, Karen always tries to be helpful. She wants to go to a good college like Vassar or Smith and plans everything she does carefully, with this in mind. At LeMoyen everybody feels that she has a real chance to get into the kind of college she would like to go to.

7. Mill and Jill Bernstein.

Mill and Jill Bernstein are two of the craziest kids you can imagine, crazy in a great way, that is. While they aren't really twins they look so much alike that they might as well be. It really gets you, you never know which one you're talking to, and they are always pulling gags on people that way. They've got so much talent they can do anything and almost do. They both play instruments in the band, they have their own vocal duet, and they are really wonderful with their mimicry. They are a must at any party because they usually make it go. At LeMoyen, they're for the school all the way, the real boosters. They're the in-everything girls, cheerleading, the school paper, debating, the works. They also run everything; they should, too, because they get things done. Right now Mill is organizing the senior class trip, and Jill is chairing the Junior Clambake Committee. LeMoyen has a lot to thank Mill and Jill for, and it's going to remember them for a long time.

    8. Nicky Galetti.

For the past three years the right side of the line of the LeMoyen football team has been practically impregnable. The reason is right tackle, Nicky Galetti, two hundred and twenty pounds of solid bone and muscle. Nicky is a great team man, hard-working, and loyal, and never an angry word. This year Nicky played every minute of every game, except for the last two in the game with City High. It was really Nick's game, and against LeMoyen's traditional foes, too. Nicky led the offense, and on defense he was, as usual, the key man. Unfortunately, LeMoyen's backfield was weak this year, and the game was scoreless until the last few minutes when Nicky blocked a City punt. Joe White recovered it for a touch-

Table 5. Students' Card Choices for *The King's Visit*

	Card Pile Placement	Best	Good	Neutral	Poor	Worst	GAPP
(6)	Karen Clarke	109	91	35	9	2	2.6
(3)	Elfrieda Eubanks	60	116	57	12	1	2.0
(7)	Bernstein sisters	36	70	104	30	6	0.9
(8)	Nicky Galetti	9	52	119	56	10	− 0.1
(5)	Ronnie, Big Joe, and Pink	10	49	113	60	14	− 0.2
(1)	Nancy Harris	0	41	123	68	14	− 0.5
(9)	Scott Cowen	10	31	87	90	28	− 0.9
(4)	Johnny Adams	9	26	64	106	41	− 1.3
(2)	Eric Pratt	3	16	36	61	130	− 2.5
	Sum (N = 246)	246	492	738	492	246	

down. Everybody felt that it was too bad that it wasn't Nicky, just so he could have scored at least once. When the coach took him out a few minutes later, the stands went mad cheering for him—a great team man if there ever was one.

9. Scott Cowen.

Scott Cowen is supposed to be a genius. When he was twelve years old his parents arranged for him to take a special course in mathematics at the university nearby, and he did very well indeed. Although all the other students in the course were either specially selected senior high school students or college freshmen, Scott came out first in the class. According to the instructor's report, "Mr. Cowen is potentially a mathematician of the first order and with proper training should be able in the future to do work of great significance." At LeMoyen, Scott has continued to do well. His entries in the Senior High School Division Science Fair won first prize both last year and this. He is a brilliant chess player and managed a draw with the state champion. And he is editor of the LeMoyen *Xantippe,* the school literary magazine. Scott's work at LeMoyen is always original and always competent, although it does tend to be sloppy. He's sloppy, also, in the way he dresses,

Table 6. Teachers' Card Choices for *The King's Visit*

Card Pile Placement	Best	Good	Neutral	Poor	Worst	GAPP
(6) Karen Clarke	20	17	13	5	0	2.0
(3) Elfrieda Eubanks	13	25	13	4	0	1.4
(7) Bernstein sisters	8	12	25	10	0	0.7
(5) Ronnie, Big Joe, and Pink	3	13	30	7	2	0.3
(1) Nancy Harris	2	16	21	14	2	0.1
(8) Nicky Galetti	3	13	19	14	6	− 0.3
(9) Scott Cowen	3	9	18	21	4	− 0.6
(4) Johnny Adams	3	3	18	25	6	− 1.2
(2) Eric Pratt	0	2	8	10	35	− 2.9
Sum (N = 55)	55	110	165	110	55	

and he does manage to argue with some of the teachers. If it wasn't for this he would probably be valedictorian of his class. He has the ability to be.

Episode V—Miss Post's English Assignment

Miss Elsie Post is, by consensus, the finest teacher LeMoyen has and probably ever has had. Her subject is English, and her skill lies in drawing the best out of even the most reluctant student. Under her guidance young people develop a real interest for literature, no matter what their background, and for many of them her class is the first time in their lives in which they have attempted seriously to express their thoughts with style and distinction. Miss Post is often gay and sometimes even frivolous while teaching, but underneath there is a resolute spirit. She is stern and surprisingly demanding in her assignments. "You know, she expects the impossible," is an often-heard student comment the first day of class. Yet, when the year is over, many own up that she'd gotten that impossible. "It makes you feel proud to do well for Miss Post," is the way Ronnie Jackson said it to Scott Cowen one day, while they were working at putting *Xantippe* together for publication. "Yeah," answered Scott, "I never thought I'd go for poetry and all that stuff, but after you've heard about it from her, and then read some of it, well, it's great, it's something she does that makes it real."

Miss Post is just as demanding of herself as she is of her students. She spends hours each day correcting class themes and homework assignments. And she has a reputation for uncovering each and every error the thoughtless, ignorant, or deceitful student has let slip into his work—this despite her advanced age and notably weak eyesight. Her comments on the papers are in themselves something of a form of art, always precise and to the point, and yet affectionate, amusing, interesting, and, where necessary, devastating. As the students at LeMoyen soon discover, Miss Post is not an easy person to fool.

Miss Post has taught at LeMoyen for many, many years. A number of the parents of the present student body had her as a teacher when they attended LeMoyen, and they always seem to remember her much as she is today. However, Eric Pratt, exercising a scientific bent he generally kept well under wraps, found her picture in the 1934 annual, and announced, much to his surprise he claimed, that she had once been a most attractive lady. After Eric's discovery had gained currency throughout the school, rumors of a tragic love were rife around LeMoyen, but nothing was ever proven. Whatever her private life, though, Miss Post must always have been a very good teacher. For, only last summer while attending a summer basketball clinic at a famous eastern university, Mr. Regan met an eminent scientist who, on hearing of LeMoyen, asked about Miss Elsie Post, his once-upon-a-time teacher. The scientist then went on to say that she was the finest teacher he had ever had, bar none, and this despite his many years of education in college and graduate school.

Assume that you are a student in Miss Post's class. Today she told her class that each member was to bring to class tomorrow several lines of poetry which he felt best expressed what *love* means to him. She indicated that the students would be expected to read and discuss their selections in class the next day. Assume further that it is evening, and you have come up with nine possible selections. They are:

1. Yet in herself she dwelleth not,
   Although no home were half so fair;
   No simplest duty is forgot,
   Life hath no dim and lowly spot
   That doth not in her sunshine share.

   She doeth little kindnesses,
   Which most leave undone, or despise;
   For naught that sets one heart at ease,
   And giveth happiness or peace,
   Is low-esteemed in her eyes.

   She hath no scorn of common things,
   And, though she seems of other birth,
   Round us her heart intwines and clings,
   And patiently she folds her wings
   To tread the humble path of earth.

2.   True love's the gift which God has given
     To man alone beneath the heaven;
     It is not fantasy's hot fire,
     Whose wishes, soon as granted, fly;
     It liveth not in fierce desire,
     With dead desire it doth not lie;
     It is the secret sympathy,
     The silver link, the silken tie,
     Which heart to heart and mind to mind
     In body and in soul can bind.

3.   No man is an island,
     No man stands alone,
     Each man's joy is joy to me,
     Each man's grief is my own.[2]

4.   No thorns go as deep as the rose's
     And love is more cruel than lust,
     Time turns the old days to derision,
     Our loves into corpses or wives;
     And marriage and death and division
     Make barren our lives.

5.   When our two souls stand up erect and strong,
     Face to face, silent, drawing nigh and nigher.

6.   He prayeth best who loveth best
     All things both great and small;
     For the dear God who loveth us,
     He made and loveth all.

7. Breathes there the man, with soul so dead,
Who never to himself hath said,
This is my own, my native land!
Whose heart hath ne'er within him burn'd
As home his footsteps he hath turned,
From wanderings on a foreign strand?

8. There is a pleasure in the pathless woods,
There is a rapture on the lonely shore,
There is a society, where none intrudes,
By the deep sea and music in its roar;
I love not man the less, but Nature more.

9. Ah, love, let us be true
To one another! for the world, which seems
To lie before us like a land of dreams,
So various, so beautiful, so new.
Hath really neither joy, nor love, nor light,
Nor certitude, nor peace, nor help for pain;
And we are here as on a darkling plain
Swept with confused alarms of struggle and flight
Where ignorant armies clash by night.

Episode VI—Alan Slade and His Friends

Early in his senior year, Alan Slade, a short, well-proportioned boy who is captain of the tennis team at LeMoyen High School and has been an honor student through his whole high school career, began to run into trouble. His grades have fallen off sharply, though they are leveling off at a point well above passing. He has been seen around town in one or two taverns that have records of violating the law against selling liquor to minors, and which the principal of the school has been trying unsuccessfully to have permanently closed. He was picked up a few weeks ago for drunken driving, but the lab test showed an alcohol content just below that necessary to establish intoxication. His father, a lawyer with a reputation for sharp legal technique, was quick to point this out and prevent the boy from being formally charged. But he also forbade him the use of either of the Slade cars for an indefinite period, until "he got himself straightened out." Not being able to drive now,

Table 7. Students' Selections of Poems for *Miss Post's English Assignment*

Card Pile Placement	Best	Good	Neu-tral	Poor	Worst	GAPP	Sigma
(2) True love's the gift (Scott—*The Lay of the Last Minstrel*)	77	77	76	12	3	1.9	2.0
(6) He prayeth best (Coleridge—*The Ancient Mariner*)	49	77	89	23	7	1.2	2.2
(3) No man is an island (the popular ballad; a paraphrase on a *Devotion* by Donne)	37	100	65	31	12	1.1	2.3
(8) There is a pleasure (Byron—*Childe Harold's Pilgrimage*, Canto IV)	19	69	87	61	9	0.2	2.3
(1) Yet in herself she (James Russell Lowell —*To Love*)	23	39	122	49	12	0.1	2.1
(7) Breathes there the man (Scott—*The Lay of the Last Minstrel*)	9	50	83	81	22	− 0.5	2.3
(9) Ah, love, let us be true (Arnold—*Dover Beach*)	12	35	67	88	43	− 1.1	2.4
(5) When our two souls (E. B. Browning—*Sonnets from the Portuguese*)	12	21	94	74	44	− 1.1	2.1
(4) No thorns go as deep (Swinburne—*Dolores*)	7	22	52	71	93	− 1.9	2.0
Sum (N = 245)	245	490	735	490	245		

Alan seems to spend most of his time hanging around the house or a candy store near the school that few students patronize, not doing much of anything. His tennis game is shot, and so are LeMoyen's chances for the year.

Nobody seems to know just how Alan's trouble started, though Monica St. Loup, another senior who is a cheerleader and president of the girls' Panhellenic council, has hinted to several of her intimate friends that she does know, although she would rather not talk about it. She did, however, overcome her aversion to doing so long enough to go to Mr. Blakely, Dean of Boys, and plead for help for Alan before anyone else had even noticed that there was anything wrong with him. Despite his encouragements—"The kids all know my door is always open," Mr. Blakely has often said—not many LeMoyen students feel free to go to the dean unless sent for. But the Dean of Boys is also, *ex officio,* in charge of student activities at LeMoyen. Mr. Blakely's admiration for Monica St. Loup is well known in the school. "Monica is about as close to an All-American girl as you can get," Mr. Blakely observed once. "Pretty as a picture; smart, too; any group she's in seems always to have a lot of fun. But her mother doesn't have to worry about her a bit; Monica can be trusted. She knows just how far she can go and not lose her self-respect. If this school had more like her, my job would be easy."

It was to Mr. Blakely, then, that Monica turned; not on her own behalf, but on that of Alan Slade. The discussion was, of course, confidential; but immediately afterward Mr. Blakely sent, separately, for Johnny Barto, a junior with a bad reputation in school as a troublemaker, and for Alan. Mr. Blakely took no formal action, but when Johnny left school that day he never came back. Some of the kids say he has left town; he has certainly not been seen around school. To Alan, Mr. Blakely spoke gently but firmly, if somewhat ambiguously. "I'm here to help you, son," he said. "I think you know that. This kind of situation isn't a disciplinary matter; intelligent people don't think of it that way any more, really. But you do need professional help. During the year, you'll be applying for college; then there's the army to think of; these people count on us to be honest with them about the emotional adjustment of our students. You have such a good record here, Alan, and I'm going to see to it that you don't spoil it. I don't even want you to worry about it, son; normal growth is our business."

Mr. Blakely's tone became less warm, however, when Alan insisted, and continued to insist more and more anxiously, that he did not understand what Mr. Blakely was talking about. "It would be better, son," said Mr. Blakely, "if you could trust me. It would be better if you could trust *yourself;* the only way out is to face up to this like the man we hope you will become. The first step is to be absolutely honest; and that is what you'll have to do. I'll tell you what we'll do. I'm going to set up an appointment for you with Dr. Bruch" (the visiting school psychiatrist for the LeMoyen district) "when he comes next month. I'm not a psychiatrist, and I don't pretend to be. But I am Dean of Boys here; and I am responsible for your well-being and for that of the other boys you are in contact with here. Until we get this report—and I'm afraid Dr. Bruch is a pretty busy man—I'll do what I can for you. Meanwhile, don't worry."

This was three months ago. Whether or not Alan took Mr. Blakely's advice not to worry, he is, as has been stated, in trouble now. Dr. Bruch's report, when received, recommended regular psychotherapy; but the school has no program for providing this. Mr. and Mrs. Slade, when Mr. Blakely told them of Dr. Bruch's recommendation, were uncooperative and ungrateful. "I'm afraid you interpret your responsibility and your mandate both too broadly and too loosely," Mr. Slade replied. "I'm not certain that I know what you are talking about any better than Alan does; but if I do I can well understand your vagueness, since you are quite right in supposing that a more forthright statement would be libelous." "If we *should* think—as we do not—that our son needed psychiatric help," Mrs. Slade added, "we would send him to our own analyst. Dr. Liebig has kept our marriage going for twenty years, which is a tribute to his competence if not to his judgment. We know that Alan has been miserable at school this year, and we have been worried sick about him; but we didn't know what was wrong and he doesn't seem to be able to tell us. Now that you've told us what you've put him through, we can begin to understand it. All we ask of you is that you attend to his education, which seemed to be going pretty well, by your own account, until you brought all this up."

Here, however, Mr. Blakely was adamant. His responsibility, he said, extended to all aspects of the welfare of LeMoyen boys while they were in school. Mr. and Mrs. Slade could ignore Dr. Bruch's recommendation if they chose; but if they did he would insist that Alan report to him for a weekly conference, at which "I'll try to help him as much as he will let me." Otherwise, he would be forced to recommend to the principal that young Slade be suspended from school, "without prejudice, for reasons of health." So far, there have been six of these conferences. During them, after polite greetings, Alan sits silently, while Mr. Blakely waits patiently "for you to get tired, Alan, of your resistance."

No one at LeMoyen supposes that Monica St. Loup asked Mr. Blakely to help Johnny Barto also. Nor did she. Monica's usually inexhaustible good will never extended to young Barto, except for a brief period early last year when Monica did try to take an interest in him. "He could amount to something, you know," she said to one of her sorority sisters who had warned her against getting "mixed up" with Johnny. "He's bright, even if he is a couple of years older than the other boys in his class. That's just his background. And he's attractive, in a kind of feline way, like a tiger. He could learn, if he had somebody to take him in hand. Don't worry about me. It's Alan you ought to be worrying about. He's such a sweet boy; and so shy; I really wish I knew how to help him. I've tried, but I can't seem to reach him, somehow. I'm sure he hasn't any idea what he's getting into."

But Monica had no more success with Johnny than with Alan. The two boys were discussing her, rather casually, late one night during a camping trip, which they often took together. "You watch out for her, Shrimpboat," Johnny told Alan. "She isn't what she thinks she is. Oh, she's all for good clean fun, and no passes accepted. But just fail to make them when she expects them, and see what happens. I know."

Monica was not the only one who disapproved of the friendship between the two boys. Mrs. Slade had also complained about it to her husband, but he had disagreed with her. "I can't go along with that, dear," he said. "If you'll remember, Johnny's grandfather just about got my career started for me; though if Johnny knows it, he never said anything to Alan. There was always a streak of the gentleman in those Bartos. Oh, they have no talent for legitimacy, and the whole line has just gone to hell since repeal; it was probably a blessing the old man got bumped off when he did. There was nothing any lawyer could have done for Johnny's father; and I'm glad he didn't come to me. But there's plenty of people jumped all over the boy since he's been down; and you know, I don't think we'd like to join them. Alan can take care of himself as well as I could at his age; and he'll have to, won't he, against people more dangerous than Johnny Barto?"

1. Bad off as he seems to be, the root of Alan's trouble is probably basically self-pity. Certainly, he is lucky at least to have both a friend and a counselor so devoted to helping him. If he won't let them, he can't expect things to get much better.

2. The attitude of Alan's parents illustrates how necessary it is that parents cooperate with the school, if as much as possible is to be done for students when they need help. In a world as interdependent as ours, the individual must cooperate with the legitimate institutions of society if progress is to be made.

3. Neurotic parents rear neurotic children: this is the iron law of psychoanalysis. The older Slades' hostility to getting any psychiatric help for their son is but an extension of their guilt for the entire situation.

4. At the heart of Mr. Blakely's attitude is essentially middle-class prejudice. If Johnny Barto were Alan's social equal, their friendship would appear perfectly natural to him.

5. The worst thing that can be said about Mr. Blakely's policy in this case is that it is too soft and compromising. Knowing what he evidently does—or he wouldn't have dared to go this far—he ought to have kicked both these young punks out of town, rather than just one. Of course, under the circumstances, he has to watch his step legally.

6. Mr. Blakely seems to be on the right track; but the school's resources do not extend far enough to back him up. When the

school psychiatrist recommends that a student be given psychiatric help, the school should require that he accept it and, if necessary, provide the funds for facilities to make it possible.

7. Mr. Blakely's action is both unprofessional and a gross invasion of privacy. He is allowing himself to be influenced by one student against another, has used his office to break up a private friendship between two students, and done grave injury to both. To call this "helping" is either hypocrisy or lunacy.

8. The most remarkable factor in the situation is the Slades' wonderfully democratic and tolerant attitude. Despite their apparent wealth and success, they recognize that a boy with Johnny's background should be encouraged to make something out of himself and, despite their misgivings, permit their son to befriend him closely. This is the kind of thing that America means.

9. The most hopeful factor in the situation, so far as Alan is concerned, is that his parents basically respect and care for him so much and can still say no when they have to, both to him and to the school authorities. Nobody is proof against fools, busybodies, or a woman scorned; but with this kind of homelife to draw on, Alan will probably come through, scars and all.

Table 8. Students' Card Choices for *Alan Slade and His Friends*

Card Pile Placement	Best	Good	Neutral	Poor	Worst	GAPP
(2) Cooperate with school	106	88	42	6	3	2.5
(1) Bad off as	29	119	65	27	5	1.3
(6) Right track	41	94	61	41	8	1.1
(3) Neurotic parents	11	49	114	49	22	− 0.2
(9) The most hopeful	21	40	98	67	19	− 0.2
(8) The most remarkable	8	39	130	48	20	− 0.3
(4) At the heart of	9	34	110	73	19	− 0.6
(7) Invasion of privacy	20	19	64	87	55	− 1.3
(5) Young punks	0	8	51	92	94	− 2.4
Sum (N = 245)	245	490	735	490	245	

Selective
Bibliography

Adorno, T. W., *et al. The Authoritarian Personality*. New York: Harper & Row, Publishers, Inc., 1950.

Anderson, Harold H. (ed.). *Creativity and Its Cultivation*. New York: Harper & Row, Publishers, Inc., 1959.

Becker, Howard S. "The Career of the Chicago Public School Teacher," *American Journal of Sociology,* 57 (1952), 470-477.

———. "The Teacher in the Authority System of the Public School," *Journal of Educational Sociology,* 27 (1953), 128-141.

Bettelheim, Bruno, and Morris Janowitz. *The Dynamics of Prejudice*. New York: Harper & Row, Publishers, Inc., 1950.

Bruner, Jerome S. *The Process of Education*. New York: Vintage Books, 1960.

Buber, Martin. *I and Thou*. New York: Charles Scribner's Sons, 1958.

———. "Productivity and Existence," in *Identity and Anxiety, Survival of the Person in Mass Society*. M. R. Stein, A. J. Vidich, and D. M. White (eds.). Glencoe: The Free Press, 1960, pp. 628-632.

Cremin, Lawrence A. *The Genius of American Education*. New York: Vintage Books, 1966.

Desan, Wilfrid. *The Marxism of Jean-Paul Sartre*. New York: Doubleday & Co., Inc., 1965.

Dewey, John. *Moral Principles in Education*. New York: Philosophical Library, 1959.

Erikson, Erik H. (ed.). *The Challenge of Youth*. New York: Anchor Books, 1965.

Friedenberg, Edgar Z. *The Vanishing Adolescent*. New York: Dell Publishing Co., 1959.

———. *Coming of Age in America: Growth and Acquiescence*. Random House, Inc., 1965.

Fromm, Erich. *Man for Himself: An Inquiry into the Psychology of Ethics*. New York: Holt, Rinehart & Winston, Inc., 1947.

Getzels, Jacob W., and Philip W. Jackson. *Creativity and Intelligence*. New York: John Wiley & Sons, Inc., 1962.

Goffman, Erving. *Asylums*. New York: Anchor Books, 1961.

Gold, Hilary A. "Sociometry and the Teacher," *International Journal of Sociometry and Sociatry,* III, 3-4 (1963), 65-71.

———. "Training Teachers for the Gifted," *Gifted Child Quarterly,* 7 (Autumn, 1963), 93-97.

Goodman, Paul. *Growing Up Absurd.* New York: Random House, Inc., 1960.

Guilford, J. P., "Creativity," *American Psychologist,* 5 (1950), 444-454.

———. "The Structure of Intellect," *Psychological Bulletin,* 53 (July, 1956), 267-293.

———. *Personality.* New York: McGraw-Hill Book Co., 1959.

Henry, Jules. "Attitude Organization in Elementary School Classrooms," *American Journal of Orthopsychiatry,* 28 (1957), 117-133.

———. "Working Paper on Creativity," *Harvard Educational Review,* 27 (1957), 148-155.

———. *Culture Against Man.* New York: Random House, Inc., 1963.

Holt, John. *How Children Fail.* New York: Pitman Publishing Corp., 1964.

Kubie, L. S. *Neurotic Distortion of the Creative Process.* New York: Noonday Press, 1961.

Laing, R. D., and D. G. Cooper. *Reason and Violence, A Decade of Sartre's Philosophy, 1950-1960.* London: Tavistock Publications, 1964.

Lipset, Seymour M. *Political Man: The Social Bases of Politics.* New York: Doubleday & Co., Inc., 1960.

Miel, Alice (ed.). *Creativity in Teaching.* Belmont, Calif.: Wadsworth Publishing Co., Inc., 1961.

Musgrove, F. *Youth and the Social Order.* Bloomington, Ind.: The University of Indiana Press, 1965.

Nordstrom, Carl, and Edgar Z. Friedenberg. *Why Successful Students in the Natural Sciences Abandon Careers in Science.* New York: Brooklyn College, 1961.

———, and Hilary A. Gold. *Influence of Ressentiment on Student Experience in Secondary School.* New York: Brooklyn College, 1965.

Pace, C. Robert and George Stern. *A Criterion Study of College Environment.* New York: Syracuse University Research Institute, 1958.

Riesman, David, with Nathan Glazer and Reuel Denney. *The Lonely Crowd: A Study of the Changing American Character.* New Haven, Conn.: Yale University Press, 1961.

Sartre, Jean-Paul. *Being and Nothingness.* Translated and with an introduction by Hazel E. Barnes. New York: Philosophical Library, 1956.

———. *Search for a Method.* New York: Alfred A. Knopf, Inc., 1963.

Scheler, Max. *Ressentiment.* Translated by William W. Holdheim, with an introduction by Lewis A. Coser. Glencoe: The Free Press, 1961.

Schrag, Peter. *Voices in the Classroom.* Boston: Beacon Press, Inc., 1965.

Torrance, E. Paul. *Guiding Creative Talent.* Englewood Cliffs, N. J.: Prentice-Hall, Inc., 1962.

————. *Rewarding Creative Behavior.* Englewood Cliffs, N. J.: Prentice-Hall, Inc., 1965.

Index

CARL NORDSTROM obtained his A.B. from Antioch, his M.A. from C
University, and his Ph.D. from the New School for Social Resea
is currently Associate Professor of Economics at Brooklyn College
he has been teaching since 1949. Professor Nordstrom is also the
(with Friedenberg) of *Why Successful Students of the Natural Sc
Abandon Careers in Science* and (with Friedenberg and Gold) of
ence of Ressentiment on Student Experience in Secondary School.

EDGAR Z. FRIEDENBERG received his B.S. from Centenary College, his M
from Stanford University, and his Ph.D. from the University of Chica
He has taught at the University of Chicago and Brooklyn College, and
now Professor of Sociology at the University of California at Davi
Professor Friedenberg is the author of *The Vanishing Adolescent, Comin*
of Age in America: Growth and Acquiescence, and *The Dignity of Youth*
and Other Atavisms.

HILARY A. GOLD acquired his A.B. and M.S. from Brooklyn College and his
Ed.D. from Teachers College, Columbia University. He is Assistant
Professor of Education at Brooklyn College, where he has been teaching
since 1960. Professor Gold has taught in the public schools and has had
both administrative and teaching experience in curriculum development
on both the public school and college levels. He is the author of a number
of research studies on education and a frequent contributor to journals
such as *Group Psychotherapy, The Journal of Experimental Education,*
and *Gifted Child Quarterly.*